50 Italian Classics

STEP-BY-STEP
50 Italian Classics

Consultant Editor
Gabriella Rossi

LORENZ BOOKS

First published in the UK by Lorenz Books in 1998

© 1998 Anness Publishing Limited

Lorenz Books is an imprint of
Anness Publishing Limited
Hermes House
88–89 Blackfriars Road
London SE1 8HA

This edition published in 1998 for Index

ISBN 1 85967 630 8

A CIP catalogue record is available from the British Library

Publisher: Joanna Lorenz
Project editor: Alison Macfarlane
Editor: Ruth Baldwin
Designer: Brian Weldon
Recipes: Carla Capalbo, Jacqueline Clarke, Frances Cleary, Roz Denny,
Joanna Farrow, Sarah Gates, Shirley Gill, Christine Ingram, Norma MacMillan,
Elizabeth Martin, Kate Whitman, Jenni Wright,
Photographers: Karl Adamson, Steve Baxter, Michelle Garrett, Amanda Heywood,
Patrick McLeavey, Michael Michaels

Printed in Hong Kong

1 3 5 7 9 10 8 6 4 2

For all recipes, quantities are in both metric and imperial
measures, and, where appropriate, measures are also given in standard
cups and spoons. Follow one set, but not a mixture, because they are
not interchangeable.

CONTENTS

INTRODUCTION

Italian cooking is strongly regional – the dishes of Florence, Venice, Genoa, Piedmont, Rome and Naples all have their own character. This is largely because Italy was not unified until 1861, and although the regions are now more able (and willing) to share their natural produce, they still rely heavily on what they can grow themselves. Sun-ripened tomatoes, aubergines and peppers feature strongly in the cookery of the south, fish is the staple food on the coast, Parmesan cheese is at its best in Parma, dairy products are used in much of the cookery of the north (with, for example, butter replacing olive oil in many of the dishes) and the best beef is reared in Tuscany. Each area has its "classic" dish – Milan has its creamy risotto, Bologna its tagliatelle with meat sauce, Naples its pizza and Rome its lamb cooked with anchovies and herbs.

Despite the diversity of Italian cooking the one unifying factor is the freshness of the ingredients. Produce is bought daily, sometimes even twice daily, from the local market. Dishes are often very simple – meats and fish are grilled or roasted, sauces often take no longer than the pasta to cook and delicious pizzas can be created in minutes – allowing the quality of the ingredients to do the work.

Olive oil plays a vital role in Italian cooking, used in nearly every recipe, from a simple salad tossed with extra virgin olive oil vinaigrette, to a classic tomato sauce for pasta or the warm and crusty bread served with every meal. It is rich in monounsaturated fats, helping to contribute to the healthy diet Italians eat; supported by lots of low-fat carbohydrate in the form of pasta and rice and freshly picked vegetables.

Italians love their food and they love sharing it with friends and family. They take time in its preparation and time in its eating. All the delicious and authentic recipes in this book will help to capture the Italian enthusiasm for food, whether you choose to serve a simple salad or an elaborate meal.

The Italian meal

One of the many attractions of the Italian meal is the relaxed way in which it is eaten and enjoyed. Most meals in Italy start with a plate of antipasti, particularly if pasta is not being served as a course. It could simply contain a selection of delicious olives, but will more usually include a variety of cold roasted or marinated vegetables, cold meats such as prosciutto or Parma ham, and delicious breads such as ciabatta and focaccia to mop up the juices. It could also include some hot crostini – rounds of baked bread topped with melting cheese and various garnishes – or mini pizzas. Whatever the choice, a good quality olive oil is of the utmost importance.

Salads
Salads also feature in antipasti, but apart from the basic green salad, most can, by varying the portions, be served at any meal, as a starter, an accompaniment or even as a main course.

Soups
Soups are popular in Italy, although they are not usually eaten at the same meal as rice or pasta as they often contain these ingredients. When soup is served as a separate course, however, it is in hearty portions. The most substantial soups are served as a main course as a light alternative for the main meal of the day.

Vegetables
Vegetables rarely accompany meat, chicken or game; a few potatoes and a green salad are considered plenty after a first course of pasta or rice. Instead vegetables are usually eaten as a separate dish, either in small quantities as a first course, or in larger quantities as a main course. Many – green beans, artichoke hearts, peppers – are also popular ingredients in Italian salads.

Pasta and rice
Pasta eaten in southern Italy and rice eaten in the north are both traditionally served after the antipasti as a first course before the main course of fish or meat. But pasta and rice dishes can be eaten as any part of a meal and at any time of day.

Polenta
Polenta, another Italian staple, is normally eaten with a main course to soak up the juices or added to hearty dishes baked in the oven.

Cheese
Cheese, if it is eaten at all at a meal, is served after the main course. It is usually a limited choice and is sometimes accompanied by a sweet pear or a ripe peach. It is also added to pizzas and some sauces, while grated Parmesan is frequently served with pasta dishes.

Desserts
Although Italians love sweet food, everyday meals are normally concluded with fresh fruit. You are much more likely to see Italians eating cakes and pastries with a cup of coffee in the morning or afternoon. Elaborate desserts are kept for special occasions, often bought rather than made, and sensibly left to the skilled hands of the pastry cook.

Right: *In Italy it is the freshness of the vegetables, often bought at market on the day they are used, that makes the food so delicious.*

Equipment

Many of the utensils in the Italian kitchen are everyday items found in most kitchens, but some specialized ones are particularly useful. Pasta can be made by hand, but a pasta machine will make it much lighter work, and trying to serve spaghetti from the pan without a special spoon is very frustrating. If you are making pizzas, a cutting wheel will cut them into clean slices.

earthenware pot

Biscuit cutter
Usually used for cutting biscuit dough into fancy shapes but is equally good for cutting fresh pasta shapes.

Colander
Indispensable for draining hot pasta and vegetables.

Earthenware pot
Excellent for slow-cooking stews, soups or sauces. It can be used either in the oven or on top of the stove on a gentle heat with a metal heat diffuser under it to prevent cracking. Many shapes and sizes are available. To season a terracotta pot before using it for the first time, immerse it in cold water overnight. Remove from the water and rub the unglazed bottom with a garlic clove. Fill with water and bring slowly to the boil. Discard the water. Repeat the process, changing the water, until the "earth" taste disappears.

Fluted pastry cutter
For cutting fresh pasta or pastry.

Hand food mill
Excellent for soups, sauces and tomato "passata": the pulp

passes through the holes, leaving the seeds and skin behind.

Ice cream scoop
Better for firm and well-frozen ice creams.

Icing nozzles
For piping decorations, garnishes, etc. Use with a nylon or paper pastry bag.

Italian ice cream scoop
Good for soft ices that are not too solid.

Meat hammer
Good for pounding escalopes. It can also be used to crush nuts and whole spices.

Olive stoner
Can be used for stoning olives or cherries.

Palette knife
Very useful for spreading and smoothing.

Parmesan cheese knife
In Italy Parmesan is not cut with a conventional knife, but broken off the large cheese wheels using this kind of wedge. Insert the point and apply pressure.

Pasta machine
Many models are available, including sophisticated electric and industrial models. Most have an adjustable roller width and thin and wide noodle cutters.

Pasta rolling pin
A length of dowelling 5 cm/2 in in diameter can also be used. Smooth the surface with fine sandpaper before using for the first time.

Pestle and mortar
For hand-grinding spices, rock salt, pepper, herbs and breadcrumbs.

Pizza cutting wheel
Useful for cutting slices, although a sharp knife may also be used.

Spaghetti spoon
The wooden "teeth" catch the spaghetti strands as they boil.

Whisk
Excellent for smoothing sauces and beating egg whites.

Wide vegetable peeler
Very easy to use for peeling all sizes of vegetable.

ice cr scoo

Italian ice cream scoop

pasta machi

wide vegetable peeler

icing nozzle

pestle and
mortar

pasta
rolling pin

hand food mill

olive stoner

fluted
pastry
cutter

whisk

biscuit
cutter

meat
hammer

colander

spaghetti spoon

Parmesan
cheese
knife

pizza cutting
wheel

palette knife

Basic Ingredients

Cured Meats

Cured meats are a popular ingredient of antipasti, and each region has its own specialities. A typical antipasto could consist of a plate of mixed prepared meats and sausages. Salamis, pancetta, air-dried bresaola, coppa and mortadella sausages are some of the meats most commonly used in Italy, often served with crusty bread and butter. Prosciutto crudo, raw Parma ham, is the most prized of all meats, and is delicious served thinly sliced with ripe melon or fresh figs.

Cheeses

An Italian meal is more likely to end with a selection of cheeses and fruit than a sweet dessert. Among the huge variety of cheeses, the following are some of the best known:

Gorgonzola
This creamy blue cheese is made in Lombardy. It has a mild flavour when young, which becomes stronger with maturity.

Mascarpone
This is a rich, triple-cream cheese with a mild flavour. It is often used in desserts as a substitute for whipped cream.

Mozzarella
Mozzarella is a fresh, white cheese made from water buffalo's or, more commonly, cow's milk. The texture is soft and chewy and the taste mild.

Parmesan
Parmesan is a long-aged, full-flavoured cheese with a hard rind, used for both grating and eating in slivers. The large wheels are aged from between 18 to 36 months. Fresh Parmesan is superb, and is incomparably better than the ready-grated varieties sold pre-packed in jars.

Pecorino
There are two main types of Pecorino, Pecorino Romano and Pecorino Toscano, both made from ewe's milk. This salted, sharp-flavoured cheese is widely used for dessert eating, and for grating when mature.

Scamorza
A distinctive-shaped cheese made from cow's milk. Its shape is due to being hung from a string during ageing.

Gorgonzola

Scamorza

Parmesan cheese

Parma ham

bresaola

mozzarella

Pecorino

mortadella

cacciatoro

salami

pancetta

Storecupboard Ingredients

The following ingredients are all commonly used to give Italian dishes their characteristic flavours and they are good basics to keep in your storecupboard for use when you need them.

Amaretti biscuits
Usually served with sweet wine, for dipping.

Balsamic vinegar
This has only recently become widely available outside Italy. Aged slowly in wooden barrels, the finest varieties are deliciously mellow and fragrant. The taste is quite sweet and concentrated, so only a very little is needed.

Capers
Aromatic buds pickled in jars of wine vinegar. They go well with garlic and lemon.

Dried chillies
Good for adding spicy flavour to all kinds of dishes.

Fennel seeds
These have a great affinity with fish, pork and poultry and can also be sprinkled on bread.

Juniper berries
These have a sweet, resinous flavour that goes well with hearty meat dishes.

Olive oil
Perhaps the single most important ingredient in a modern Italian kitchen is olive oil. The fruity flavour of a fine extra virgin olive oil perfumes any dish it is used in, from pesto sauce to the simplest salad dressing. Buy the best olive oil you can afford: one bottle goes a long way and makes a huge difference to any recipe.

Olives
These are one of Italy's most wonderful native ingredients. Unfortunately, fresh cured olives do not travel well, and many of the most delicious varieties are not available outside the Mediterranean. Sample canned or bottled olives before adding to sauces as they sometimes acquire an unpleasant metallic taste that could spoil the flavour of the dish. Good quality olives can be bought from the fresh food counters of supermarkets and at delicatessens.

Pine nuts
These are very popular in the Mediterranean region and are an essential ingredient in pesto sauce. They can be used in sweet and savoury dishes.

Polenta
The coarsely ground yellow maize is a staple of the northern Italian diet. It can be eaten hot or left to cool and set, then sliced and brushed with oil before grilling.

Porcini mushrooms
These mushrooms are found in the woods in various parts of Europe in autumn. They can be eaten cooked fresh, or sliced thinly and dried in the sun or in special ovens. A few dried porcini soaked in water add a deliciously woodsy flavour.

Pulses
A typical Italian storecupboard will always contain a supply of dried, natural ingredients. Dried beans and lentils should be stored in air-tight containers for use in soups and stews.

Rice
Another popular ingredient in northern Italy is rice, which is used to make risotto. Of the special varieties grown in the area for this purpose, the best known are arborio, vialone nano and carnaroli.

Sun-dried tomatoes
Ready packed in oil, they can be used straight from the jar in salads, sauces and stuffings.

white peppercorns

polenta

fennel seeds

jun
be

green olives

bay leaves

salt cod

sun-dried
tomatoes

olive oil

balsamic
vinegar

garlic

red chillies

arborio rice

green lentils

chick-peas

porcini
mushrooms

cannellini beans

pinto beans

capers

amaretti biscuits

pine nuts

coffee beans

Fresh Produce

Italian cooking is based on the creative use of fresh, seasonal ingredients. Vegetables and herbs play central roles in almost every aspect of the menu. In the markets, there is a sense of anticipation at the beginning of each new season, heralded by the arrival, on the beautifully displayed stalls, of the year's first artichokes, olives, chestnuts or wild mushrooms. Seasonal recipes come to the fore and make the most of available produce.

Regional differences

The cuisine of the hot south is typically Mediterranean: vegetables feature in pasta dishes, on their own or in salads. In the cooler north, meat dishes are more plentiful and there is a vast array of dairy products. Central Italy combines the best of both north and south. The one thing that all the regions have in common is that they take the best, freshest ingredients and cook them very simply. Italian cuisine is not a complicated or sophisticated style of cooking.

Vegetables

Many of the vegetables once considered exotically Mediterranean are now readily available in the markets and supermarkets of most countries. Fennel and aubergines, peppers, courgettes and radicchio are now increasingly present in pasta sauces, soups and pizzas, as well as adding a wonderful accent to meat and fish.

Wherever you shop, look for the freshest possible fruits and vegetables. Choose unblemished, firm, sun-ripened produce, preferably locally or organically grown.

Herbs

Many herbs grow freely in the Mediterranean climate, especially basil, parsley, thyme, marjoram, oregano, sage and rosemary, and they are used extensively in Italian cooking.

Fresh herbs such as basil, parsley and sage are easy to cultivate in window boxes and gardens and have an infinitely finer flavour than their dried counterparts.

If buying and using dried herbs, store them in a cool dark place and don't keep them for too long or they will become stale and musty.

Right, clockwise from top left: *garlic cloves, artichokes, red onions, red cauliflower, fennel, radicchio, fresh herbs (basil, thyme, parsley and sage), aubergines and green peppers.*

Basic Pasta Dough

Allow 200 g/7 oz/1¾ cups plain white
(all-purpose) flour, pinch of salt and 15 ml/
1 tbsp olive oil to 2 eggs (size 2) for 3–4 servings,
depending on the required size of portion.

1 Sift the flour and salt on to a clean work surface and make a well in the centre with your fist.

2 Pour the beaten eggs and oil into the well. Gradually mix the eggs into the flour with your fingers.

3 Knead the pasta until smooth, wrap and allow to rest for at least 30 minutes before attempting to roll out. The pasta will be much more elastic after resting.

Using a Food Processor

1 Sift the flour into the bowl and add a pinch of salt.

2 Pour in the beaten eggs and oil and chosen flavouring, if using, and process until the dough begins to come together. Tip out the dough and knead until smooth. Wrap the dough and leave to rest for 30 minutes. Use as required.

Using a Pasta Machine

1 Feed the rested dough several times through the highest setting first, then reduce the settings until the required thickness is achieved.

2 A special cutter will produce fettuccine or tagliatelle. A narrower cutter will produce spaghetti or tagliarini.

Basic Pizza Dough

This simple bread base is rolled out thinly for a traditional pizza recipe.

Makes one of the following:
1 x 25–30 cm/10–12 in round pizza base
4 x 13 cm/5 in round pizza bases
1 x 30 x 18 cm/12 x 7 in oblong

INGREDIENTS
175 g/6 oz/1½ cups strong
   white flour
1.25 ml/¼ tsp salt
5 ml/1 tsp easy-blend dried yeast
120–150 ml/4–5 fl oz/½–⅔ cup
   lukewarm water
15 ml/1 tbsp olive oil

dried yeast

strong white flour

olive oil

1 Sift the flour and salt into a large mixing bowl.

2 Stir in the yeast.

3 Make a well in the centre of the dry ingredients. Pour in the water and oil and mix with a spoon to a soft dough.

4 Knead the dough on a lightly floured surface for about 10 minutes until smooth and elastic.

5 Place the dough in a greased bowl and cover with clear film. Leave in a warm place to rise for about 1 hour or until the dough has doubled in size.

6 Knock back the dough. Turn on to a lightly floured surface and knead again for 2–3 minutes. Roll out as required and place on a greased baking sheet. Push up the edge to make a rim. The dough is now ready for topping.

Basic Tomato Sauce for Pizzas

Tomato sauce forms the basis of the topping in many pizza recipes. Make sure it is well seasoned and thick before spreading it over the base. It will keep fresh in a covered container in the refrigerator for up to 3 days.

*Covers 1 x 25–30 cm/
10–12 in round or
30 x 18 cm/12 x 7 in
oblong pizza base*

INGREDIENTS

15 ml/1 tbsp olive oil
1 medium onion, finely chopped
1 garlic clove, crushed
400 g/14 oz can chopped
    tomatoes
15 ml/1 tbsp tomato purée
15 ml/1 tbsp chopped fresh
    mixed herbs, such as parsley,
    thyme, basil and oregano
pinch of sugar
salt and ground black pepper

1 Heat the oil in a saucepan, add the onion and garlic and gently fry for about 5 minutes or until softened.

2 Add the tomatoes, tomato purée, herbs, sugar and seasoning.

3 Simmer, uncovered, stirring occasionally, for 15–20 minutes or until the tomatoes have reduced to a thick pulp. Leave to cool.

Basic Tomato Sauce for Pasta

Tomato sauce is without a doubt the most popular dressing for pasta in Italy. This sauce is best made with fresh tomatoes of any variety, but also works well with canned plum tomatoes.

Serves 4

INGREDIENTS
60 ml/4 tbsp olive oil
1 medium onion, very finely
    chopped
1 garlic clove, finely chopped
450 g/1 lb tomatoes, fresh
    or canned, chopped, with
    their juice
a few fresh basil leaves or
    parsley sprigs
salt and ground black pepper

1 Heat the oil in a medium saucepan. Add the onion, and cook over moderate heat for 5–8 minutes or until it is translucent.

2 Stir in the garlic, fresh tomatoes and 45 ml/3 tbsp water. If using canned tomatoes, add them with their juice instead of water and break them up with a wooden spoon. Season with salt and pepper and add the herbs. Cook for 20–30 minutes.

3 Pass the sauce through a food mill or purée in a food processor. To serve, reheat gently, adjust the seasoning, if necessary, and pour the sauce over the drained pasta.

Bolognese Meat Sauce

This great meat sauce is a speciality of Bologna. It is delicious with tagliatelle or short pasta such as penne or conchiglie as well as spaghetti, and is indispensable in baked lasagne.

Serves 6

INGREDIENTS
25 g/1 oz/2 tbsp butter
60 ml/4 tbsp olive oil
1 medium onion, finely chopped
25 g/1 oz/2 tbsp pancetta
    or unsmoked bacon,
    finely chopped
1 carrot, finely sliced
1 celery stick, finely sliced
1 garlic clove, finely chopped
350 g/12 oz lean minced beef
150 ml/¼ pint/⅔ cup red wine
120 ml/4 fl oz/½ cup milk
400 g/14 oz can plum tomatoes,
    chopped, with juice
1 bay leaf
1.5 ml/¼ tsp fresh thyme leaves
salt and ground black pepper

butter   olive oil   onion

pancetta   carrot

garlic   celery

minced beef   milk   red wine

bay leaf   thyme   canned tomatoes

COOK'S TIP
This sauce keeps well in the refrigerator for several days and can also be frozen.

1 Heat the butter and oil in a heavy saucepan. Add the onion and cook gently for 3–4 minutes. Add the pancetta or bacon and cook until the onion is translucent. Stir in the carrot, celery and garlic. Cook for 3–4 minutes until the vegetables are softened.

2 Add the beef and crumble it into the vegetables with a fork. Stir until the meat loses its red colour. Season with salt and pepper. Pour in the wine, raise the heat slightly and cook for 3–4 minutes until the liquid evaporates. Add the milk and cook until it evaporates.

3 Stir in the tomatoes with their juice and the herbs. Bring the sauce to the boil. Reduce the heat to low, and simmer, uncovered, for 1½–2 hours, stirring occasionally. Adjust the seasoning, if necessary, before serving.

Chopping herbs

Use this method to chop herbs until they are as coarse or as fine as you wish.

1 Strip the leaves from the stalk and pile them on a chopping board.

2 Using a sharp knife, cut the herbs into small pieces, holding the tip of the blade against the board and rocking the blade back and forth.

Pasta and Chick-pea Soup

A thick soup from central Italy. The addition of a sprig of fresh rosemary provides a typically Mediterranean flavour.

Serves 4–6

INGREDIENTS

200 g/7 oz/1 cup chick-peas
3 garlic cloves, peeled
1 bay leaf
90 ml/6 tbsp olive oil
50 g/2 oz/¼ cup salt pork, pancetta
   or bacon, diced
1 sprig fresh rosemary
150 g/5 oz ditalini or other short
   hollow pasta
salt and ground black pepper
freshly grated Parmesan cheese, to
   serve (optional)

garlic

chick-peas

Parmesan cheese

olive oil

bay leaf

rosemary

pancetta

ditalini

COOK'S TIP

Leave the soup to stand for about 10 minutes before serving. This will allow the flavour and texture to develop.

1 Soak the chick-peas in water overnight. Rinse well and drain. Place the chick-peas in a large saucepan with water to cover. Bring to the boil and boil for 15 minutes. Rinse and drain.

2 Return the chick-peas to the pan. Add water to cover, one of the garlic cloves, the bay leaf, 45 ml/3 tbsp of the oil and a pinch of pepper.

3 Simmer for about 2 hours until tender, adding more water as necessary. Remove the bay leaf. Pass about half the chick-peas through a food mill or purée in a food processor with a few tablespoons of the cooking liquid. Return the purée to the pan with the rest of the peas and the remaining cooking water.

4 Sauté the diced pork, pancetta or bacon gently in the remaining oil with the rosemary and remaining garlic cloves until just golden. Discard the rosemary and garlic.

5 Stir the pork with its oil into the chick-pea mixture.

6 Add 600 ml/1 pint/2½ cups of water to the chick-peas, and bring to the boil. Adjust the seasoning if necessary. Stir in the pasta and cook until just *al dente*. Serve with the Parmesan handed separately, if desired.

Tomato and Fresh Basil Soup

A soup for late summer, when fresh tomatoes are at their most flavoursome.

Serves 4–6

INGREDIENTS

15 ml/1 tbsp olive oil
25 g/1 oz/2 tbsp butter
1 medium onion, finely chopped
900 g/2 lb ripe Italian plum
    tomatoes, roughly chopped
1 garlic clove, roughly chopped
about 750 ml/1¼ pints/3 cups
    chicken or vegetable stock
120 ml/4 fl oz/½ cup dry white wine
30 ml/2 tbsp sun-dried tomato paste
30 ml/2 tbsp shredded fresh
    basil, plus a few whole leaves
    to garnish
150 ml/¼ pint/⅔ cup double cream
salt and pepper

olive oil *garlic* *chicken stock*
butter *onion*
double cream
white wine *basil*
plum tomatoes *sun-dried tomato paste*

VARIATION

The soup can also be served chilled. Pour it into a container after sieving and chill for at least 4 hours. Serve in chilled bowls.

1 Heat the oil and butter in a large saucepan over a medium heat until foaming. Add the onion and cook gently for about 5 minutes, stirring frequently, until it is softened but not brown.

2 Stir in the chopped tomatoes and garlic, then add the stock, white wine and sun-dried tomato paste, with salt and pepper to taste. Bring to the boil, then lower the heat, half-cover the pan and simmer gently for 20 minutes, stirring occasionally to stop the tomatoes sticking to the base of the pan.

3 Process the soup with the shredded basil in a blender or food processor, then press through a sieve into a clean pan.

4 Add the double cream and heat through, stirring. Do not allow the soup to approach boiling point. Check the consistency and add more stock if necessary, then adjust the seasoning. Pour into heated bowls and garnish with whole basil leaves. Serve at once.

Roasted Plum Tomatoes with Garlic

These are so simple to prepare, yet taste absolutely wonderful. Use a large, shallow earthenware dish that will allow the tomatoes to sear and char in a hot oven.

Serves 4

INGREDIENTS
8 plum tomatoes
12 garlic cloves
60 ml/4 tbsp extra virgin olive oil
3 bay leaves
salt and ground black pepper
45 ml/3 tbsp fresh oregano leaves,
  to garnish

plum tomatoes

olive oil

garlic

oregano   *bay leaves*

1 Preheat the oven to 230°C/450°F/Gas 8. Halve the plum tomatoes, leaving a small part of the green stem intact for decoration.

2 Select an ovenproof dish that will hold all the tomatoes snugly in a single layer. Place the tomatoes in the dish with the cut side facing upwards, and push the whole, unpeeled garlic cloves between them.

3 Brush the tomatoes with the oil, add the bay leaves and sprinkle black pepper over the top.

4 Bake for about 45 minutes until the tomatoes have softened and are sizzling in the dish. They should be charred around the edges. Season with salt and a little more black pepper, if needed. Garnish with the fresh oregano leaves and serve immediately.

VARIATION
For a sweet alternative, use red or yellow peppers instead of the tomatoes. Cut each pepper in half and remove all the seeds before placing, cut side up, in an ovenproof dish.

COOK'S TIP
Select ripe, juicy tomatoes without any blemishes to get the best flavour out of this dish.

Roasted Peppers in Oil

Peppers take on a delicious, smoky flavour if roasted in a very hot oven. The skins can easily be peeled off and the flesh stored in olive oil. This oil can then be used to add extra flavour to salad dressings.

Makes one small jar

INGREDIENTS
6 large peppers of differing colours
450 ml/¾ pint/1¾ cups olive oil

peppers

olive oil

COOK'S TIP
These pepper slices make very attractive presents, especially around Christmas time. You can put them in special preserving jars, available from kitchen equipment shops. Alternatively re-use large jam jars: first wash them thoroughly, soaking off the labels at the same time. Sterilize all jars before use by placing them upside down in a low oven for about half an hour. While the jars are still hot add the sliced peppers, and fill with a good olive oil. Cover immediately with the lid and fix on an attractive label.

1 Preheat the oven to the highest temperature: about 230°C/450°F/Gas 8. Lightly grease a large baking sheet.

2 Quarter the peppers, remove the cores and seeds then squash them flat with the back of your hand. Lay the peppers skin side up on the baking sheet.

3 Roast the peppers at the top of the oven for about 12–15 minutes until the skins blacken and blister.

4 Remove the peppers from the oven, cover with a clean tea towel until they are cool, then peel off the skins.

5 Slice the peppers and pack them into a clean sterilized preserving jar. Add the olive oil to the jar to cover the pepper slices completely, then seal the lid tightly.

6 Store the peppers in the refrigerator and use them within 2 weeks. Use the oil in salad dressing or for cooking once the peppers have been eaten.

Artichokes with Garlic and Herb Butter

It is fun eating artichokes and even more fun to share one between two people. You can always have a second one to follow so that you get your fair share!

Serves 4

INGREDIENTS
2 large or 4 medium
    globe artichokes
salt

FOR THE GARLIC AND HERB BUTTER
75 g/3 oz/6 tbsp butter
1 garlic clove, crushed
15 ml/1 tbsp chopped fresh
    mixed herbs

butter

garlic

mixed herbs

globe artichokes

1 Wash the artichokes well in cold water. Using a sharp knife, cut off the stalks level with the bases. Cut off the top 1 cm/½ in of leaves. Snip off the pointed ends of the remaining leaves with scissors and discard.

2 Put the prepared artichokes in a large saucepan of lightly salted water. Bring to the boil, cover and cook for about 40–45 minutes or until one of the lower leaves comes away easily from the choke when gently pulled.

3 Drain upside down for a couple of minutes while making the sauce. Melt the butter over a low heat, add the garlic and cook for 30 seconds. Remove from the heat, stir in the herbs and then pour into one or two small serving bowls.

4 Place the artichokes on individual serving plates and serve with the garlic and herb butter.

COOK'S TIP
To eat an artichoke, pull off each leaf and dip into the garlic and herb butter. Scrape off the soft, fleshy base with your teeth. When the centre is reached, pull out the hairy choke and discard it, as it is inedible. The base can be cut up and eaten with the remaining garlic butter.

Asparagus with Prosciutto

When asparagus is young and tender, you need do nothing more than trim off the ends of the stalks. However, larger spears, with stalk ends that are tough and woody, require some further preparation before cooking.

Serves 4

INGREDIENTS
675–900 g/1½–2 lb medium
   asparagus spears
175 g/6 oz/¾ cup clarified butter
   (see Cook's Tip)
10 ml/2 tsp lemon juice
30 ml/2 tbsp finely chopped spring
   onions
15 ml/1 tbsp finely chopped fresh
   parsley
4 slices prosciutto
salt and ground black pepper

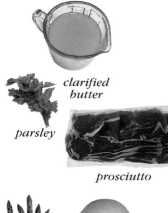

clarified butter

parsley

prosciutto

asparagus

lemon

spring onions

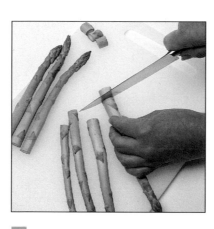

1 Cut off the tough, woody ends of the asparagus and trim the spears so that they are all about the same length.

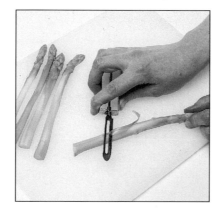

2 If you like, remove the skin. Lay a spear flat and hold it just below the tip. With a vegetable peeler, shave off the skin, working lengthways down the spear to the end of the stalk. Roll the spear over so that you can remove the skin from all sides.

3 Half-fill a large frying pan with salted water. Bring to the boil, add the asparagus and simmer for 4–5 minutes or until it is just tender. (Pierce a stalk to test.) Remove and drain.

4 Combine the clarified butter, lemon juice, spring onions and parsley in a small saucepan. Season with salt and pepper to taste. Heat the herb butter until it is just lukewarm.

5 Divide the asparagus among four warmed plates. Drape a slice of prosciutto over each portion. Spoon the herb butter over the top and serve.

COOK'S TIP

To clarify butter, heat until it stops bubbling. Remove from the heat and leave to stand until the sediment has sunk to the bottom. Gently pour off the fat and strain it through muslin.

Insalata Tricolore

This can be a simple starter if served on individual salad plates, or part of a mixed dish of appetizers laid out on a platter. When lightly salted, tomatoes make their own flavoursome dressing with their natural juices.

Serves 4–6

Ingredients

1 small red onion, thinly sliced
6 large full-flavoured tomatoes
extra virgin olive oil, for sprinkling
50 g/2 oz/1 small bunch rocket or
    watercress, roughly chopped
175 g/6 oz mozzarella cheese, sliced
    thinly or grated
30 ml/2 tbsp pine nuts (optional)
salt and ground black pepper

*large
tomatoes*

*extra virgin
olive oil*

pine nuts

*small red
onion*

*mozzarella
cheese*

rocket

1 Soak the onion slices in a bowl of cold water for 30 minutes, then drain and pat dry. Skin the tomatoes by slashing them with a sharp knife and dipping briefly in boiling water.

2 Slice the tomatoes and arrange half the slices on a large platter, or divide them between small plates if you prefer.

3 Sprinkle liberally with olive oil, then layer with half the chopped rocket or watercress and onion slices, seasoning well. Add half the cheese, sprinkling over more oil and seasoning as you go.

4 Repeat with the remaining tomato slices, salad leaves, cheese and oil.

5 Season well to finish and complete with some oil and a good scattering of pine nuts, if using. Cover the salad and chill for at least 2 hours before serving.

Variation

Instead of the fresh rocket or watercress, use chopped fresh basil which goes particularly well with the flavour of ripe tomatoes.

Mixed Seafood Salad

All along Italy's coasts versions of this salad appear. Use fresh seafood that is in season, or use a combination of fresh and frozen.

Serves 6–8

INGREDIENTS
350 g/12 oz small squid
1 small onion, cut into quarters
1 bay leaf
200 g/7 oz uncooked prawns,
   in their shells
750 g/1½ lb fresh mussels, in
   their shells
450 g/1 lb fresh small clams
175 ml/6 fl oz/¾ cup white wine
1 fennel bulb

FOR THE DRESSING
75 ml/5 tbsp extra virgin olive oil
45 ml/3 tbsp lemon juice
1 garlic clove, finely chopped
salt and ground black pepper

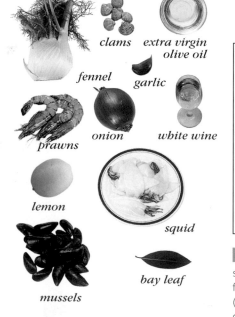

clams   *extra virgin olive oil*

fennel   *garlic*

prawns   *onion*   *white wine*

lemon   *squid*

mussels   *bay leaf*

1 Working near the sink, clean the squid. Peel off the thin skin from the body section. Rinse well. Pull the head and tentacles away from the sac section. Some of the intestines will come away with the head. Remove and discard the translucent quill and any remaining insides from the sac.

2 Cut off the tentacles and remove the small beak from the base. Discard the head and intestines. Rinse the sac and tentacles under cold running water. Drain. Bring a large pan of water to the boil. Add the onion and bay leaf and cook the squid for 10 minutes, until tender. Remove with a slotted spoon, cool, then slice the sac into rings 1 cm/½ in wide. Cut each tentacle in half. Set aside.

3 Drop the prawns into the same boiling water used for the squid, and cook for about 2 minutes or until they turn pink. Remove with a slotted spoon. Peel and devein. (The cooking liquid may be strained and kept for soup.) Cut off the "beards" from the mussels. Scrub and rinse the mussels and clams well in several changes of cold water.

4 Put the mussels and clams in a large saucepan with the wine. Cover and steam for about 5 minutes until the shells open (discard any that do not). Remove the opened mussels with a slotted spoon.

5 Shell the clams and the mussels. Chop the fennel top and reserve for the dressing. Chop the bulb into bite-size pieces and put in a bowl with the clams, mussels, squid and prawns.

6 Make the dressing by mixing the oil, lemon juice, garlic and chopped fennel top in a bowl. Add salt and pepper to taste. Pour over the salad and toss well. Serve immediately.

Baked Onions with Sun-dried Tomatoes

This wonderfully simple vegetable dish of baked onions brings together the flavours of a hot Italian summer – tomatoes, fresh herbs and olive oil.

Serves 4

INGREDIENTS
450 g/1 lb small onions, peeled
10 ml/2 tsp chopped fresh rosemary
    or 5 ml/1 tsp dried rosemary
2 garlic cloves, chopped
15 ml/1 tbsp chopped fresh parsley
120 ml/4 fl oz/½ cup sun-dried
    tomatoes in oil, drained and
    chopped
90 ml/6 tbsp olive oil
15 ml/1 tbsp white wine vinegar
salt and ground black pepper

olive oil

garlic

rosemary

sun-dried tomatoes

small onions

white wine vinegar

parsley

1 Preheat the oven to 150°C/300°F/ Gas 2. Grease a shallow baking dish. Drop the onions into a saucepan of boiling water and cook for 5 minutes. Drain in a colander.

2 Spread the onions in the bottom of the prepared baking dish.

VARIATIONS
Other herbs can be used instead of the rosemary and parsley in this dish. Try using shredded fresh basil which will enhance the flavour of the sun-dried tomatoes, or fresh thyme, which complements the flavour of baked onions perfectly. If you can find small red onions, these would make a nice change, or even mix the two colours.

3 Combine the rosemary, garlic, parsley, salt and pepper in a small mixing bowl and sprinkle the mixture evenly over the onions in the dish.

4 Scatter the sun-dried tomatoes over the onions. Drizzle the olive oil and vinegar on top.

5 Cover the dish with a sheet of foil and bake for 45 minutes, basting occasionally. Remove the foil and bake for about 15 minutes more until the onions are golden brown all over. Serve immediately from the dish.

Grilled Aubergine Parcels

These are delicious little Italian bundles of tomatoes, Mozzarella cheese and basil, wrapped in slices of aubergine.

Serves 4

INGREDIENTS
2 large, long aubergines
225 g/8 oz mozzarella cheese
2 plum tomatoes
16 large basil leaves
30 ml/2 tbsp olive oil
salt and ground black pepper

FOR THE DRESSING
60 ml/4 tbsp olive oil
5 ml/1 tsp balsamic vinegar
15 ml/1 tbsp sun-dried tomato paste
15 ml/1 tbsp lemon juice

FOR THE GARNISH
30 ml/2 tbsp pine nuts, toasted
torn basil leaves

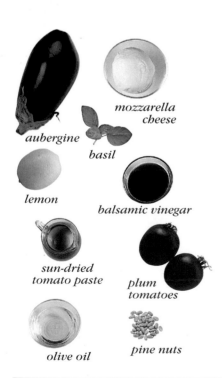

aubergine

mozzarella cheese

basil

lemon

balsamic vinegar

sun-dried tomato paste

plum tomatoes

olive oil

pine nuts

1 To make the dressing, whisk together the olive oil, vinegar, sun-dried tomato paste and lemon juice. Season to taste and set aside.

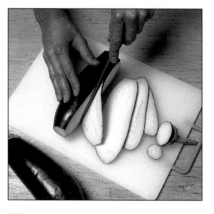

2 Remove the stalks from the aubergines and cut the aubergines lengthways into thin slices – the aim is to get 16 slices in total (each about 5 mm/ ¼ in thick), disregarding the first and last slices. (If you have a mandolin, it will cut perfect, even slices for you; otherwise use a sharp long-bladed knife.)

3 Bring a large pan of salted water to the boil and cook the aubergine slices for about 2 minutes or until just softened. Drain the sliced aubergines, then dry on kitchen paper. Set aside.

4 Cut the cheese into slices. Cut each tomato into eight slices, not counting the first and last slices.

5 Take two aubergine slices and place on a baking sheet or in a large flameproof dish, forming a cross. Place a slice of tomato in the centre of each cross, season with salt and pepper, then add a basil leaf, followed by a slice of cheese, another basil leaf, a slice of tomato and more seasoning.

6 Fold the ends of the aubergine slices around the cheese and tomato filling to make a neat parcel. Repeat with the rest of the assembled ingredients to make eight parcels. Chill the parcels for about 20 minutes.

7 Preheat the grill. Brush the parcels with olive oil and cook for about 5 minutes on each side or until golden. Serve hot, with the dressing, and sprinkled with pine nuts and basil.

Courgettes with Onion and Garlic

Use a good-quality olive oil and sunflower oil. The olive oil gives the dish a delicious fragrance without overpowering the courgettes.

Serves 4

INGREDIENTS
15 ml/1 tbsp olive oil
15 ml/1 tbsp sunflower oil
1 large onion, chopped
1 garlic clove, crushed
4–5 medium courgettes, cut into
    1 cm/½ in slices
150 ml/¼ pint/⅔ cup chicken or
    vegetable stock
2.5 ml/½ tsp chopped fresh oregano
salt and ground black pepper
chopped fresh parsley, to garnish

garlic

courgettes

olive oil

chicken stock

sunflower oil

oregano

onion

parsley

1 Heat the olive and sunflower oils in a large frying pan and fry the onion and garlic over a moderate heat for 5–6 minutes until the onion has softened and is beginning to brown.

2 Add the sliced courgettes and fry for about 4 minutes until they just begin to be flecked with brown, stirring frequently.

3 Stir in the stock, oregano and seasoning and simmer gently for 8–10 minutes or until the liquid has almost evaporated.

4 Spoon the courgettes into a warmed serving dish, sprinkle with chopped parsley and serve.

COOK'S TIP
Courgettes are very popular in Italy, grown in many kitchen gardens. They make a lovely summer dish, taking very little time to prepare. If you can find them, choose small courgettes, which tend to be much sweeter than the larger ones.

Stuffed Peppers

Sweet peppers can be stuffed and baked with many different fillings, from leftover cooked vegetables to rice or pasta. Blanching the peppers first helps to make them tender.

Serves 6

INGREDIENTS

6 medium to large peppers, any colour
200 g/7 oz/1 cup rice
60 ml/4 tbsp olive oil
1 large onion, finely chopped
3 canned anchovy fillets, chopped
2 garlic cloves, finely chopped
3 medium tomatoes, peeled and cut into small dice
60 ml/4 tbsp white wine
45 ml/3 tbsp finely chopped fresh parsley
115 g/4 oz/½ cup mozzarella cheese, cut into small dice
90 ml/6 tbsp freshly grated Parmesan cheese
salt and pepper
Basic Tomato Sauce (see Basic Recipes), to serve (optional)

peppers
olive oil
anchovy fillets
white wine
rice
tomato sauce
onion
garlic
mozzarella cheese
Parmesan cheese
parsley
tomatoes

COOK'S TIP
Choose peppers with a sturdy, even base, so that they will stand on end unsupported in the baking dish. This will make them easier to cook and serve.

1 Cut the tops off the peppers. Scoop out the seeds and core. Blanch the peppers and their tops in a large pan of boiling water for 3–4 minutes. Remove and stand upside down on racks to drain.

2 Boil the rice according to the instructions on the packet, but drain and rinse it in cold water 3 minutes before the recommended cooking time has elapsed. Drain again.

3 In a large frying pan, heat 30 ml/ 2 tbsp of the oil and sauté the onion until soft. Stir in the anchovy pieces and the garlic and mash them. Add the tomatoes and the wine and cook for 5 minutes.

4 Preheat the oven to 190°C/375°F/ Gas 5. Remove the tomato mixture from the heat. Stir in the rice, parsley, mozzarella and 60 ml/4 tbsp of the Parmesan cheese. Season the mixture with salt and pepper.

5 Pat the insides of the peppers dry with kitchen paper. Sprinkle with salt and pepper. Stuff the peppers with the tomato and rice mixture. Sprinkle the tops with the remaining Parmesan and the remaining oil.

6 Arrange the peppers in a shallow baking dish. Pour in enough water to come 1 cm/½ in up the sides of the peppers. Bake for 25 minutes. Serve at once, with tomato sauce if desired. These peppers are also good served at room temperature.

Radicchio and Chicory Gratin

Radicchio and chicory take on a different flavour when cooked in this way. The creamy béchamel combines wonderfully with the bitter leaves.

Serves 4

INGREDIENTS
2 heads radicchio
2 heads chicory
120 ml/4 fl oz/½ cup sun-dried
    tomatoes in oil, drained
    and roughly chopped,
    oil reserved
salt and ground black pepper

FOR THE SAUCE
25 g/1 oz/2 tbsp butter
15 g/½ oz/2 tbsp plain flour
250 ml/8 fl oz/1 cup milk
pinch of grated nutmeg
50 g/2 oz/½ cup grated
    Emmenthal cheese
chopped fresh parsley,
    to garnish

radicchio

Emmenthal cheese

butter

chicory

sun-dried tomatoes

plain flour

milk

nutmeg

parsley

1 Preheat the oven to 180°C/350°F/ Gas 4. Grease a 1.2 litre/2 pint/5 cup baking dish. Trim the radicchio and chicory and discard any damaged or wilted leaves. Quarter them lengthways and arrange in the baking dish. Scatter over the sun-dried tomatoes and brush the leaves liberally with oil from the sun-dried tomato jar. Sprinkle with salt and pepper and cover with foil. Bake for 15 minutes, then remove the foil and bake for a further 10 minutes until the vegetables are softened.

COOK'S TIP

In Italy radicchio and chicory are often grilled on an outdoor barbecue. To do this, simply prepare the vegetables as above and brush with olive oil. Place cut-side down on the grill for 7–10 minutes until browned. Turn and grill for about 5 more minutes or until the other side is browned.

2 Make the béchamel sauce. Place the butter in a small saucepan and melt over a medium heat. When the butter is foaming, add the flour and cook for 1 minute, stirring. Remove from the heat and gradually add the milk, whisking all the time. Return to the heat, bring to the boil and simmer for 2–3 minutes until it thickens.

3 Season the sauce to taste and add the grated nutmeg.

4 Pour the sauce over the vegetables and sprinkle with the grated cheese. Bake for 20 minutes or until golden brown. Serve immediately, garnished with the chopped parsley.

Tuscan Baked Beans

Beans, both dried and fresh, are particularly popular in Tuscany, where they are cooked in many different ways. In this vegetarian dish the beans are flavoured with fresh sage leaves.

Serves 6–8

INGREDIENTS
600 g/1 lb 6 oz dried beans, such
   as cannellini
60 ml/4 tbsp olive oil
2 garlic cloves, crushed
3 leaves fresh sage
1 leek, finely sliced
400 g/14 oz can plum tomatoes,
   chopped, with their juice
salt and ground black pepper

cannellini beans

olive oil

garlic

canned tomatoes

leek

sage

COOK'S TIP
If fresh sage is unavailable,
use 60 ml/4 tbsp chopped fresh
parsley instead.

1 Carefully pick over the beans, discarding any stones or other particles. Place the beans in a large bowl and cover with water. Leave to soak for at least 6 hours, or overnight. Drain.

2 Preheat the oven to 180°C/350°F/ Gas 4. In a small saucepan, heat the oil and sauté the garlic cloves and sage leaves for 3–4 minutes. Remove from the heat and set aside.

3 In a large, deep baking dish combine the beans with the leek and tomatoes. Stir in the oil with the garlic and sage. Add enough fresh water to cover the beans by 2.5 cm/1 in. Mix well. Cover the dish with a lid or foil and place in the centre of the oven. Bake for 1¾ hours.

4 Remove the dish from the oven, stir the beans and season with salt and pepper. Return the beans to the oven, uncovered, and cook for another 15 minutes or until the beans are tender. Remove from the oven and allow to stand for 7–8 minutes before serving. Alternatively, leave to cool and serve at room temperature.

Malfatti with Red Sauce

If you ever felt dumplings were a little heavy, try these light spinach and ricotta malfatti instead. Serve with a tomato and red pepper sauce.

Serves 4–6

INGREDIENTS
450 g/1 lb fresh leaf spinach,
    stalks trimmed
1 small onion, chopped
1 garlic clove, crushed
15 ml/1 tbsp olive oil
400 g/14 oz/1¾ cups ricotta cheese
75 g/3 oz/1 cup dried breadcrumbs
50 g/2 oz/½ cup plain flour
5 ml/1 tsp salt
50 g/2 oz Parmesan cheese, freshly
    grated, plus slivers to garnish
grated nutmeg, to taste
3 eggs, beaten
25 g/1 oz/2 tbsp butter, melted
salt and ground black pepper

FOR THE SAUCE
1 large red pepper, seeded and
    chopped
1 small red onion, chopped
30 ml/2 tbsp olive oil
400 g/14 oz can chopped tomatoes
150 ml/¼ pint/⅔ cup water
good pinch of dried oregano
30 ml/2 tbsp single cream

spinach *onion* *ricotta cheese*
garlic
olive oil *plain flour* *eggs*
breadcrumbs
nutmeg *Parmesan cheese* *single cream* *red pepper* *butter* *red onion*
chopped tomatoes *dried oregano*

1 Blanch the spinach in the tiniest amount of water until it is limp. Drain well, pressing it in a sieve with the back of a ladle or spoon. Chop finely.

2 Lightly fry the onion and garlic in the oil for 5 minutes. Allow to cool, then mix with the spinach together with the ricotta, eggs, melted butter, breadcrumbs, flour, 5 ml/1 tsp salt, grated Parmesan and grated nutmeg to taste.

3 Mould the spinach mixture into 12 small quenelles (see Cook's Tip).

4 Meanwhile, make the sauce. Lightly sautée the red pepper and onion in the oil for 5 minutes. Add the canned tomatoes, water, oregano and seasoning. Bring to the boil then simmer gently for 5 minutes.

5 Remove the sauce from the heat and blend to a purée in a food processor. Return to the pan, then stir in the cream. Adjust the seasoning if necessary.

COOK'S TIP

Quenelles are oval-shaped dumplings. To shape the malfatti into quenelles you need two dessertspoons. Scoop up the mixture with one spoon, making sure that it is mounded up, then, using the other spoon, scoop the mixture off the first spoon, twisting the top spoon into the bowl of the second. Repeat this action two or three times until the quenelle is nice and smooth, and then gently knock it off on to a plate ready to cook. Repeat the process with the rest of the mixture.

6 Bring a shallow pan of salted water to a gentle boil, drop the malfatti into it a few at a time and poach them for about 5 minutes. Drain them well and keep them warm in a low oven.

7 Arrange the malfatti on warm plates and drizzle over the sauce. Serve topped with slivers of Parmesan.

Tomato Risotto

Creamy risotto is a classic Italian dish which can use a wide variety of ingredients, from a few simple herbs to mushrooms and seafood. Here, plum tomatoes provide a fresh, vibrant flavour and meaty texture.

Serves 4

INGREDIENTS

675 g/1½ lb firm ripe tomatoes, preferably plum
50 g/2 oz/4 tbsp butter
1 onion, finely chopped
about 1.2 litres/2 pints/5 cups vegetable stock
275 g/10 oz/1½ cups arborio rice
400 g/14 oz can cannellini beans, drained
50 g/2 oz Parmesan cheese, finely grated
salt and ground black pepper
10–12 basil leaves, shredded, and shavings of Parmesan cheese, to serve

basil   *butter*

onion

canned cannellini beans   *arborio rice*

plum tomatoes   *Parmesan cheese*   *vegetable stock*

1 Pre-heat the grill. Halve the tomatoes and scoop out the seeds into a sieve placed over a bowl. Press the seeds with a spoon to extract all the juice. Set aside.

2 Grill the tomatoes skin-side up until the skins are blackened and blistered. Leave a while until they are cool enough to handle. Gently rub off the skins using your hands and dice the flesh into even-sized pieces.

3 Melt the butter in a large pan, add the onion and cook for 5 minutes until beginning to soften. Add the tomatoes, the reserved juice and seasoning, then cook the mixture, stirring occasionally, for about 10 minutes. Meanwhile, bring the vegetable stock to the boil in another pan.

4 Add the rice to the tomatoes and stir to coat. Add a ladleful of the stock and simmer, stirring gently, until it is absorbed. Repeat, adding a ladleful of stock at a time, until all the stock is absorbed and the rice is tender and creamy.

5 Stir in the cannellini beans and finely grated Parmesan and gently heat through for a few minutes.

6 Just before serving the risotto, sprinkle each portion with shredded basil leaves and shavings of Parmesan.

Polenta with Mushrooms

This dish is delicious made with a mixture of wild and cultivated mushrooms.

Serves 6

INGREDIENTS
10 g/¼ oz/2 tbsp dried porcini
    mushrooms (omit if using
    wild mushrooms)
60 ml/4 tbsp olive oil
1 small onion, finely chopped
675 g/1½ lb mushrooms, wild
    or cultivated, or a combination
    of both
2 garlic cloves, finely chopped
45 ml/3 tbsp chopped fresh parsley
3 medium tomatoes, peeled
    and diced
15 ml/1 tbsp tomato purée
175 ml/6 fl oz/¾ cup warm water
1.5 ml/¼ tsp fresh thyme leaves,
    or 1 large pinch dried thyme
1 bay leaf
350 g/12 oz/2½ cups polenta
salt and ground black pepper
fresh parsley sprigs, to garnish

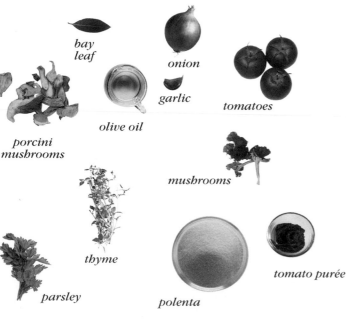

bay leaf

onion

olive oil

garlic

tomatoes

porcini mushrooms

mushrooms

thyme

tomato purée

parsley

polenta

1 Soak the dried mushrooms, if using, in a small bowl of warm water for about 20 minutes. Remove the mushrooms with a slotted spoon and rinse them well in several changes of cold water. Filter the soaking water through a layer of kitchen paper placed in a sieve and reserve.

2 In a large frying pan, heat the oil and sauté the onion over a low heat until soft and golden.

3 Clean the fresh mushrooms by wiping them with a damp cloth. Cut into slices. When the onion is soft, add the mushrooms to the pan. Stir over a medium to high heat until they give up their liquid. Add the garlic, parsley and diced tomatoes. Cook for 4–5 minutes.

4 Soften the tomato purée in the warm water (use only 120 ml/4 fl oz/ ½ cup water if using dried mushrooms). Add the purée to the pan with the herbs. Add the dried mushrooms and soaking liquid, if using, and season. Reduce the heat to low and cook for 15–20 minutes. Set aside.

5 Bring 1.5 litres/2½ pints/6¼ cups water to the boil in a large, heavy saucepan. Add 15 ml/1 tbsp salt. Reduce the heat to a simmer and begin to add the polenta in a fine rain. Stir constantly with a whisk until the polenta has all been incorporated.

COOK'S TIP
Just a few dried porcini mushrooms will help to give cultivated mushrooms a more complex and interesting flavour.

6 Switch to a long-handled wooden spoon and continue to stir the polenta over a low to medium heat until it is a thick mass and pulls away from the sides of the pan. This may take 25–50 minutes, depending on the type of polenta used. For best results, never stop stirring the polenta until you remove it from the heat. When the polenta has almost finished cooking, gently reheat the mushroom sauce.

7 To serve, spoon the polenta on to a warmed serving platter. Make a well in the centre. Spoon some of the mushroom sauce into the well, and garnish with fresh parsley sprigs. Serve at once, handing round the remaining sauce in a separate bowl.

Frittata with Sun-dried Tomatoes

Adding just a few sun-dried tomatoes gives this frittata a distinctly Mediterranean flavour.

Serves 3–4

INGREDIENTS
6 sun-dried tomatoes, dry or in oil
    and drained
60 ml/4 tbsp olive oil
1 small onion, finely chopped
pinch of fresh thyme leaves
6 eggs
50 g/2oz/½ cup freshly grated
    Parmesan cheese
salt and ground black pepper

sun-dried tomatoes

Parmesan cheese

eggs

thyme

onion

olive oil

1 Place the tomatoes in a small bowl and pour on enough hot water to just cover them. Soak for about 15 minutes. Lift the tomatoes out of the water, and slice them into thin strips. Reserve the soaking water.

2 Heat the oil in a large non-stick or heavy frying pan. Stir in the onion, and cook for 5–6 minutes or until soft and golden. Add the tomatoes and thyme. Stir over moderate heat for 2–3 minutes. Season with salt and pepper.

3 Break the eggs into a bowl and beat lightly. Stir in 45–60 ml/3–4 tbsp of the tomato soaking water and the grated Parmesan. Raise the heat under the pan.

VARIATION
Replace the sun-dried tomatoes with 50 g/2 oz/⅓ cup diced ham or prosciutto and 200 g/ 7 oz/1 cup chopped cooked spinach. When frying the onion, add a finely chopped garlic clove if you wish.

4 When the oil is sizzling, pour in the eggs. Mix them quickly into the other ingredients, and stop stirring. Lower the heat to medium and cook for about 4–5 minutes on the first side, or until the frittata is puffed and golden brown.

5 Take a large plate, place it upside down over the pan, and holding it firmly with oven gloves, turn the pan and the frittata over on to it. Slide the frittata back into the pan, and continue cooking until golden on the second side, 3–4 minutes more. Serve immediately.

Roast Monkfish with Garlic and Fennel

In the past monkfish was sometimes used as a substitute for lobster meat because it is very similar in texture. It is now appreciated in its own right and is delicious quickly roasted.

Serves 4

INGREDIENTS
1.1 kg/2½ lb monkfish tail
8 garlic cloves
15 ml/1 tbsp olive oil
2 fennel bulbs, sliced
juice and zest of 1 lemon
1 bay leaf
salt and ground black pepper

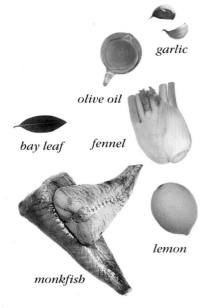

garlic

olive oil

bay leaf *fennel*

lemon

monkfish

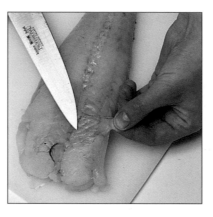

1 Preheat the oven to 220°C/425°F/ Gas 7. With a filleting knife, cut away the thin membrane covering the outside of the fish.

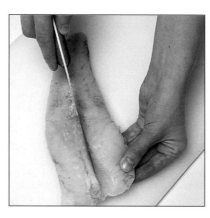

2 Cut along one side of the central bone to remove the fillet. Repeat on the other side.

3 Tie the separated fillets together with string to reshape as a tailpiece.

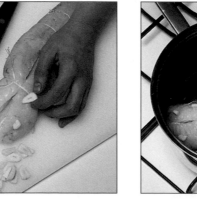

4 Peel and slice the garlic cloves and cut incisions into the fish flesh. Place the garlic slices into the incisions.

5 Heat the oil in a large, heavy-based saucepan and seal the fish on all sides.

6 Place the fish in a roasting dish together with the fennel slices, lemon juice, bay leaf and seasoning. Roast in the oven for about 20 minutes, until tender and cooked through. Serve immediately, garnished with fennel leaves and lemon zest.

COOK'S TIP
The aniseed-like flavour of fennel goes particularly well with fish. The leaves can be used as a garnish if you like.

Chargrilled Squid

If you like your food hot, chop some – or all – of the chilli seeds with the flesh. If not, cut the chillies in half lengthways, scrape out the seeds and discard them before chopping the flesh.

Serves 2

INGREDIENTS
2 whole prepared squid,
    with tentacles
75 ml/5 tbsp olive oil
30 ml/2 tbsp balsamic vinegar
140 g/5 oz/¾ cup arborio rice
2 fresh red chillies, finely chopped
60 ml/4 tbsp dry white wine
salt and pepper
fresh parsley sprigs, to garnish

squid

olive oil

white wine

balsamic vinegar

red chillies

rice

parsley

1 Make a cut down the body of each squid, then open out flat. Score the flesh with the tip of a sharp knife. Chop the tentacles. Place the squid in a glass dish. Whisk oil and vinegar. Add seasoning and pour over the squid. Cover and marinate for 1 hour. Meanwhile cook the rice in salted water until tender.

2 Heat a ridged cast-iron pan. Add the body of one of the squid. Cook over a medium heat for 2–3 minutes, pressing with a fish slice. Repeat on the other side. Cook the other body in the same way.

3 Cut the squid bodies into diagonal strips. Pile the hot risotto rice in the centre of heated soup plates and arrange the strips of squid on top. Keep hot.

4 Put the tentacles and chillies in a heavy-based frying pan. Toss over a medium heat for 2 minutes. Stir in the wine, then drizzle over the squid and rice. Garnish with parsley and serve.

Prawns in Tomato Sauce

The tomato sauce base can be sharpened up by adding hot chillies.

Serves 6

INGREDIENTS

90 ml/6 tbsp olive oil
1 medium onion, finely chopped
1 celery stick, finely chopped
1 small red pepper, seeded
    and chopped
120 ml/4 fl oz/½ cup red wine
15 ml/1 tbsp wine vinegar
400 g/14 oz can plum tomatoes,
    chopped, with their juice
1 kg/2¼ lb uncooked prawns,
    in their shells
2–3 garlic cloves, finely chopped
45 ml/3 tbsp finely chopped
    fresh parsley
1 dried chilli, crumbled or
    chopped (optional)
salt and ground black pepper

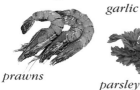

olive oil

onion

red wine

red pepper

canned plum tomatoes

celery

wine vinegar

garlic

prawns

parsley

dried chilli

1 In a heavy saucepan heat half the oil. Add the onion and cook over a low heat until soft. Stir in the celery and pepper and cook for 5 minutes. Raise the heat and add the wine, vinegar and tomatoes. Bring to the boil and cook for 5 minutes. Lower the heat, cover the pan and simmer for about 30 minutes, until the vegetables are soft.

2 Allow the vegetables to cool a little, then purée through a food mill.

3 Shell the prawns. Make a shallow incision with a small sharp knife down the centre of the back and remove the long, black vein with the tip of a knife.

4 Heat the remaining oil in a clean, heavy saucepan. Stir in the chopped garlic and parsley, plus the chilli, if using. Cook over a medium heat, stirring, until the garlic is golden. Add the prepared tomato sauce and bring to the boil.

5 Stir in the prawns. Bring the sauce back to the boil. Reduce the heat slightly and simmer until the prawns are pink and stiff: this will be about 6–8 minutes, depending on their size. Season to taste and serve on warmed plates.

Pan-fried Red Mullet with Basil and Citrus

Red mullet is popular all over the Mediterranean. This Italian recipe combines it with oranges and lemons, which grow in abundance there.

Serves 4

INGREDIENTS
4 red mullet, about
    225 g/8 oz each, filleted
90 ml/6 tbsp olive oil
10 peppercorns, crushed
2 oranges, 1 peeled and sliced and
    1 squeezed
1 lemon
30 ml/2 tbsp plain flour
15 g/½ oz/1 tbsp butter
2 canned anchovy fillets, drained
    and chopped
60 ml/4 tbsp shredded fresh basil
salt and ground black pepper

basil *lemon*

peppercorns *butter*

plain flour

orange

anchovy fillets *olive oil*

red mullet

COOK'S TIP
If you prefer, use other fish fillets for this dish, such as lemon sole, haddock or hake.

1 Place the fish fillets in a shallow dish in a single layer. Pour over the olive oil and sprinkle with the crushed peppercorns. Lay the orange slices on top of the fish. Cover the dish and leave to marinate in the refrigerator for at least 4 hours.

2 Halve the lemon, then remove the skin and pith from one half using a small sharp knife and slice thinly. Squeeze the juice from the other half.

3 Lift the fish out of the marinade and pat dry on kitchen paper. Reserve the marinade and orange slices. Season the fish with salt and pepper and dust lightly with flour.

4 Heat 45 ml/3 tbsp of the marinade in a frying pan. Add the fish and fry for 2 minutes on each side. Remove from the pan and keep warm. Discard the marinade that is left in the pan.

5 Melt the butter in the pan with any of the remaining original marinade. Add the anchovies and cook until they are completely softened.

6 Stir in the orange and lemon juice, then check the seasoning and simmer until slightly reduced. Stir in the basil. Place the fish on a warmed serving plate, pour over the sauce and garnish with the reserved orange slices and the lemon slices. Serve at once.

Baked Mussels and Potatoes

This dish originates from Puglia, noted for its imaginative baked casseroles.

Serves 2–3

INGREDIENTS
750 g/1½ lb large mussels, in
　their shells
225 g/8 oz potatoes, unpeeled
75 ml/5 tbsp olive oil
2 garlic cloves, finely chopped
8 fresh basil leaves, torn into pieces
225 g/8 oz tomatoes, peeled and
　thinly sliced
45 ml/3 tbsp breadcrumbs
salt and ground black pepper

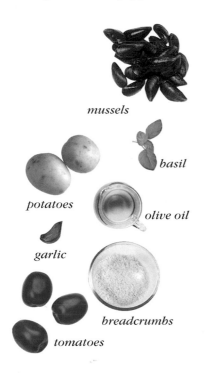

mussels

basil

potatoes

olive oil

garlic

breadcrumbs

tomatoes

1 Cut the "beards" off the mussels. Scrub and soak in several changes of cold water. Discard any with broken shells. Place the mussels with a cupful of water in a large saucepan over a medium heat. As soon as they open, lift them out. (Discard any that do not open.) Remove and discard the empty half-shells leaving the mussels in the other half. Strain any liquid in the pan through a layer of kitchen paper and reserve.

2 Boil the potatoes in salted water until they are almost cooked but still firm, then peel and slice them thinly.

3 Preheat the oven to 180°C/350°F/ Gas 4. Spread 30 ml/2 tbsp of the olive oil in the bottom of a shallow ovenproof dish. Cover with the potato slices in one layer. Add the mussels in their half-shells in one layer. Sprinkle with garlic and pieces of basil.

4 Cover with a layer of the tomato slices. Sprinkle with breadcrumbs and pepper, the filtered mussel liquid and the remaining olive oil. Bake for about 20 minutes or until the tomatoes are soft and the breadcrumbs golden. Serve directly from the baking dish.

Sea Bass en Papillote

A dramatic presentation to delight your guests. Bring the unopened parcels to the table and let them unfold their own fish to release the delicious aroma.

Serves 4

INGREDIENTS
130 g/4½ oz/generous ½ cup butter
450 g/1 lb spinach
3 shallots, finely chopped
4 small sea bass, gutted
60 ml/4 tbsp white wine
4 bay leaves
salt and ground black pepper
new potatoes and glazed carrots,
    to serve

butter

bay leaves

white wine

spinach

shallots

sea bass

new potatoes

carrots

1 Preheat the oven to 180°C/350°F/ Gas 4. Melt 50 g/2 oz/4 tbsp of the butter in a large, heavy-based saucepan, add the spinach and cook gently until almost a purée. Cool.

2 Melt another 50 g/2 oz/4 tbsp of the butter in a clean pan and add the shallots. Gently sauté for 5 minutes until soft but not browned. Add to the spinach and leave to cool.

3 Season the fish both inside and outside, then stuff the insides with the spinach and shallot filling.

4 For each fish, fold a large sheet of greaseproof paper in half and cut around the fish laid on one half, to make a heart shape when unfolded. It should be at least 5 cm/2 in larger than the fish all round. Melt the remaining butter and brush a little on to the paper. Set the fish on one side of the paper.

5 Add a little wine and a bay leaf to each fish package.

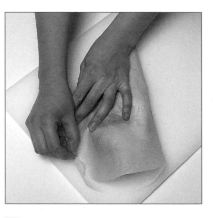

6 Fold the other side of the paper over the fish and make small pleats to seal the two edges, starting at the curve of the heart. Brush the outsides with butter. Transfer the packages to a baking sheet and bake for 20–25 minutes until the packages are brown. Serve with new potatoes and glazed carrots.

Fresh Tuna and Tomato Stew

A deliciously simple dish that relies on good basic ingredients. For real Italian flavour, serve with polenta or pasta.

Serves 4

INGREDIENTS
12 baby onions, peeled
900 g/2 lb ripe tomatoes
675 g/1½ lb fresh tuna
45 ml/3 tbsp olive oil
2 garlic cloves, crushed
45 ml/3 tbsp chopped fresh herbs
2 bay leaves
2.5 ml/½ tsp caster sugar
30 ml/2 tbsp sun-dried tomato paste
150 ml/¼ pint/⅔ cup dry white wine
salt and ground black pepper
baby courgettes and fresh herbs,
    to garnish

herbs

baby onions

garlic   *bay leaves*   *olive oil*

tomatoes

caster sugar

white wine   *tuna*

sun-dried tomato paste   *baby courgettes*

1 Leave the onions whole and cook in a pan of boiling water for 4–5 minutes until softened. Drain.

2 Slit the tomato skins and plunge the tomatoes into boiling water for 30 seconds. Refresh them in cold water. Peel away the skins and chop roughly.

VARIATION
Two large mackerel make a more readily available alternative to the tuna. Fillet them and cut into chunks or simply lay the whole fish over the sauce and cook, covered with a lid, until the mackerel is cooked through. Sage, rosemary and oregano all go extremely well with this dish. Choose whichever herb you prefer, or use a mixture.

3 Cut the tuna into 2.5 cm/1 in chunks. Heat the oil in a large frying pan and quickly fry the tuna until browned. Remove from the pan, drain and keep warm. Add the onions, garlic, tomatoes, chopped herbs, bay leaves, sugar, tomato paste and wine and bring to the boil.

4 Reduce the heat and simmer gently for 5 minutes, breaking up the tomatoes with a wooden spoon. Return the fish to the pan and cook for a further 5 minutes. Season and serve hot, garnished with baby courgettes and fresh herbs.

Stuffed Plaice Rolls

Sun-dried tomatoes, pine nuts and anchovies make a flavoursome combination for the stuffing mixture.

Serves 4

INGREDIENTS

4 plaice fillets, about 225 g/8 oz
   each, skinned
75 g/3 oz/6 tbsp butter
1 small onion, chopped
1 celery stick, finely chopped
115 g/4 oz/2 cups fresh white
   breadcrumbs
45 ml/3 tbsp chopped fresh parsley
30 ml/2 tbsp pine nuts, toasted
3–4 pieces sun-dried tomatoes in
   oil, drained and chopped
50 g/2 oz can anchovy fillets,
   drained and chopped
75 ml/5 tbsp fish stock
ground black pepper

plaice   *anchovy fillets*

fish stock   *onion*

celery   *butter*

pine nuts   *sun-dried tomatoes*

parsley

white breadcrumbs

1 Preheat the oven to 180°C/350°F/ Gas 4. Using a sharp knife, cut the plaice fillets in half lengthways to make eight smaller fillets. Melt the butter in a pan and add the onion and celery. Cover and cook over a low heat for about 15 minutes until softened. Do not allow to brown.

2 Mix together the breadcrumbs, parsley, pine nuts, sun-dried tomatoes and anchovies. Stir in the softened vegetables with the buttery juices and season with pepper to taste.

3 Divide the stuffing into eight portions. Taking one portion at a time, form the stuffing into balls, then roll up each one inside a plaice fillet. Secure each roll with a cocktail stick.

4 Place the rolls in a buttered ovenproof dish. Pour in the stock and cover the dish with buttered foil. Bake for 20 minutes or until the fish flakes. Remove the cocktail sticks. Serve the fish with some cooking juice drizzled over.

Roast Lamb with Rosemary

In Italy lamb is traditionally served at Easter. This simple roast with potatoes owes its wonderful flavour to the fresh rosemary and garlic. It makes the perfect Sunday lunch at any time of the year, served with fresh vegetables.

Serves 4

INGREDIENTS

½ leg of lamb, about 1.5 kg/3–3½ lb
2 garlic cloves, cut lengthways into thin slivers
105 ml/7 tbsp olive oil
leaves from 4 sprigs fresh rosemary, finely chopped
about 250 ml/8 fl oz/1 cup lamb or vegetable stock
675 g/1½ lb potatoes, cut into 2.5 cm/1 in cubes
a few fresh sage leaves, chopped
salt and ground black pepper
lightly cooked baby carrots, to serve

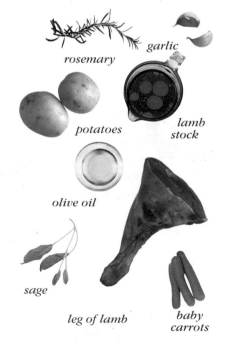

rosemary *garlic*
potatoes *lamb stock*
olive oil
sage
leg of lamb *baby carrots*

COOK'S TIP
If you like, the cooking juices can be strained and used to make a thin gravy flavoured with stock and red wine.

1 Preheat the oven to 230°C/450°F/Gas 8. Using the point of a sharp knife, make deep incisions in the lamb, especially near the bone, and insert the slivers of garlic into the holes.

4 Roast for a further 1¼–1½ hours until the lamb is tender, turning the joint two or three times more and adding the rest of the stock in two or three batches. Baste the lamb each time it is turned, to prevent the meat from drying out.

2 Put the lamb in a roasting tin and rub it all over with 45 ml/3 tbsp of the oil. Sprinkle over about half the chopped rosemary, patting it on firmly, and season with plenty of salt and pepper. Roast for 30 minutes, turning once.

5 Meanwhile, put the potatoes in a separate roasting tin and toss with the remaining oil and rosemary and the sage. Roast, on the same shelf as the lamb if possible, for 45 minutes, turning them several times until golden and tender.

3 Lower the oven temperature to 190°C/375°F/Gas 5. Turn the lamb over again and add 120 ml/4 fl oz/½ cup of the stock to the tin.

6 Transfer the lamb to a carving board, cover with a foil "tent" and leave to stand in a warm place for 10 minutes. Serve whole or carved into thin slices, surrounded by the potatoes and accompanied by carrots.

Beef Stew with Red Wine

This rich, hearty dish should be served with mashed potatoes or polenta.

Serves 6

INGREDIENTS

75 ml/5 tbsp olive oil
1.1 kg/2½ lb lean stewing beef, cut
    into 4 cm/1½ in cubes
1 medium onion, very finely sliced
2 carrots, chopped
45 ml/3 tbsp finely chopped
    fresh parsley
1 garlic clove, chopped
1 bay leaf
a few fresh thyme sprigs, or pinch
    of dried thyme
pinch of ground nutmeg
250 ml/8 fl oz/1 cup red wine
400 g/14 oz can plum tomatoes,
    chopped, with their juice
120 ml/4 fl oz/½ cup beef or
    chicken stock
about 15 black olives, stoned
    and halved
1 large red pepper, seeded and
    cut into strips
salt and ground black pepper

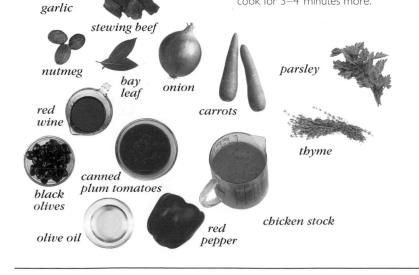

garlic
stewing beef
nutmeg
bay leaf
onion
carrots
parsley
red wine
thyme
black olives
canned plum tomatoes
chicken stock
olive oil
red pepper

1 Preheat the oven to 180°C/350°F/ Gas 4. Heat 45 ml/3 tbsp of the oil in a large, heavy, flameproof casserole. Brown the meat, a little at a time, turning it to colour on all sides. Remove each batch to a plate while the remaining meat is being browned.

2 When all the meat cubes have been browned and removed, add the remaining oil, the onion and carrots. Cook over a low heat until the onion softens. Add the parsley and garlic and cook for 3–4 minutes more.

3 Return the meat to the pan, raise the heat and stir well to mix the vegetables with the meat. Stir in the bay leaf, thyme and nutmeg. Add the wine, bring to the boil and cook, stirring, for 4–5 minutes. Stir in the tomatoes, stock and olives and mix well. Season with salt and pepper. Cover the casserole and place in the centre of the oven. Bake for 1½ hours.

4 Remove the casserole from the oven. Stir in the strips of red pepper. Return the casserole to the oven and cook, uncovered, for 30 minutes more or until the beef is tender. Serve hot.

Calves' Liver with Balsamic Vinegar

This sweet-and-sour liver dish is a speciality of Venice. Serve it very simply, with green beans sprinkled with browned breadcrumbs.

Serves 2

INGREDIENTS
15 ml/1 tbsp plain flour
2.5 ml/½ tsp finely chopped
    fresh sage
4 thin slices calves' liver, cut into
    serving pieces
45 ml/3 tbsp olive oil
25 g/1 oz/2 tbsp butter
2 small red onions, sliced and
    separated into rings
150 ml/¼ pint/⅔ cup dry
    white wine
45 ml/3 tbsp balsamic vinegar
pinch of granulated sugar
salt and ground black pepper
fresh sage sprigs, to garnish
green beans sprinkled with
    browned breadcrumbs, to serve

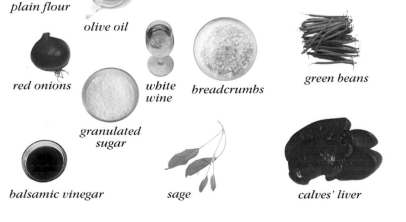

plain flour   *butter*
olive oil
red onions   *white wine*   *breadcrumbs*   *green beans*
granulated sugar
balsamic vinegar   *sage*   *calves' liver*

1 Spread out the flour in a shallow bowl. Season it with the sage and plenty of salt and pepper. Turn the liver in the flour until well coated.

2 Heat 30 ml/2 tbsp of the oil with half the butter in a wide, heavy-based saucepan or frying pan until foaming. Add the onion rings and cook gently, stirring frequently, for about 5 minutes until softened but not coloured. Remove with a fish slice and set aside.

3 Heat the remaining oil and butter in the pan until foaming, add the liver and cook over a medium heat for 2–3 minutes on each side. Transfer to heated dinner plates and keep hot.

4 Add the wine and vinegar to the pan and stir to mix with the pan juices and any sediment. Add the onions and sugar and heat through, stirring. Spoon the sauce over the liver, garnish with sage sprigs and serve at once with the green beans sprinkled with breadcrumbs.

Chicken with Chianti

Together the robust, full-flavoured red wine and red pesto give this sauce a rich colour and almost spicy flavour, while the grapes add a delicious sweetness. Serve the stew with grilled polenta or crusty bread, and accompany with rocket leaves for a contrasting hint of bitterness.

Serves 4

INGREDIENTS
45 ml/3 tbsp olive oil
4 part-boned chicken breasts, skinned
1 medium red onion
30 ml/2 tbsp red pesto
300 ml/½ pint/1¼ cups Chianti
300 ml/½ pint/1¼ cups water
115 g/4 oz red grapes, halved lengthways and seeded if necessary
salt and ground black pepper
chopped fresh parsley, to garnish
rocket leaves, to serve

chicken breasts

olive oil

Chianti

red pesto

rocket leaves

red onion

parsley

red grapes

COOK'S TIP
Use part-boned chicken breasts, if you can get them, in preference to boneless chicken for this dish as they have a better flavour. Chicken thighs or drumsticks could also be cooked in this way.

1 Heat 30 ml/2 tbsp of the oil in a large frying pan, add the chicken breasts and sauté over a medium heat for about 5 minutes until they have changed colour on all sides. Remove with a slotted spoon and drain on kitchen paper. Cut the onion in half through the root. Trim off the root, then slice the onion halves lengthways to create thin wedges.

2 Heat the remaining oil in the pan, add the onion wedges and red pesto and cook gently, stirring constantly, for about 3 minutes until the onion is softened, but not browned.

4 Reduce the heat, then cover the pan and simmer gently for about 20 minutes or until the chicken is tender, stirring occasionally.

VARIATION
Use green pesto instead of red, and substitute a dry white wine such as Pinot Grigio for the Chianti, then finish with seedless green grapes. A few spoonfuls of mascarpone cheese can be added at the end if you like, to enrich the sauce.

3 Add the Chianti and water to the pan and bring to the boil, stirring, then return the chicken to the pan and add salt and pepper to taste.

5 Add the grapes to the pan and cook over a low heat until heated through. Taste the sauce and adjust the seasoning if necessary. Serve the chicken hot with the rocket leaves and garnished with chopped parsley.

Polpettes with Mozzarella and Tomato

These Italian meat patties are made with beef and topped with mozzarella cheese and fresh tomato.

Serves 6

INGREDIENTS
½ slice white bread, crust removed
45 ml/3 tbsp milk
675 g/1½ lb minced beef
1 egg, beaten
50 g/2 oz/⅔ cup dry breadcrumbs
vegetable oil, for frying
2 beefsteak or other large
    tomatoes, sliced
15 ml/1 tbsp chopped fresh oregano
225 g/8 oz mozzarella cheese, cut
    into 6 slices
6 canned anchovy fillets, drained
    and cut in half lengthways

bread

milk

minced beef

breadcrumbs

oregano

anchovy fillets

egg

beefsteak tomatoes

vegetable oil

mozzarella cheese

1 Preheat the oven to 200°C/400°F/ Gas 6. Put the bread and milk into a small saucepan and heat very gently until the bread absorbs all the milk. Transfer the bread to a bowl, mash it to a pulp and leave to cool.

2 Put the beef into a bowl with the bread mixture, the egg and seasoning. Mix well, then shape the mixture into six patties. Sprinkle the breadcrumbs on to a plate and dredge the patties, coating them thoroughly.

3 Heat about 5 mm/¼ in oil in a large frying pan. Add the patties and fry for 2 minutes on each side until brown. Transfer to a greased ovenproof dish, in a single layer.

4 Lay a slice of tomato on top of each patty, sprinkle with oregano and season with salt and pepper. Place the mozzarella slices on top. Arrange two strips of anchovy, placed in a cross, on top of each slice of cheese.

5 Bake for 10–15 minutes until the cheese has melted and the patties are cooked through. Serve hot, straight from the dish.

Pork Steaks with *Gremolata*

Gremolata is a popular Italian garnish of garlic, citrus zest and parsley.

Serves 4

INGREDIENTS
30 ml/2 tbsp olive oil
4 pork shoulder steaks
1 medium onion, chopped
2 garlic cloves, crushed
30 ml/2 tbsp tomato purée
400 g/14 oz can chopped tomatoes
150 ml/¼ pint/⅔ cup white wine
1 bouquet garni
3 canned anchovy fillets, drained
   and chopped
salt and ground black pepper
salad leaves, to serve

FOR THE *GREMOLATA*
45 ml/3 tbsp chopped fresh parsley
grated rind of ½ lemon
grated rind of 1 lime
1 garlic clove, chopped

onion

pork steaks

garlic

tomato purée

white wine

chopped tomatoes

bouquet garni

lime

anchovy fillets

parsley

lemon

salad leaves

olive oil

1 Heat the oil in a large, flameproof casserole, add the pork steaks and brown on both sides. Remove the steaks from the casserole and set aside.

2 Add the onion to the casserole and cook until soft and beginning to brown. Add the garlic and cook for 1–2 minutes, then stir in the tomato purée, chopped tomatoes and white wine. Add the bouquet garni. Bring to the boil, then boil rapidly for 3–4 minutes to reduce and thicken slightly.

3 Return the pork to the casserole, then cover and cook for about 30 minutes. Stir in the chopped anchovies. Cover the casserole and cook for a further 15 minutes, or until the pork is tender.

4 Meanwhile, to make the *gremolata*, mix together the chopped fresh parsley, lemon and lime rinds and garlic. Set aside.

5 Remove the pork steaks and discard the bouquet garni. Reduce the sauce over a high heat, if it has not already thickened. Taste the sauce and add salt and pepper as necessary.

6 Return the pork steaks to the casserole, then sprinkle with the *gremolata*. Cover and cook for a further 5 minutes. Serve hot with salad leaves.

Veal with Tomatoes and White Wine (*Osso Bucco*)

This famous Milanese dish is rich and hearty. It is traditionally served with Risotto alla Milanese, but Tomato Risotto would go equally well.

Serves 4

INGREDIENTS
30 ml/2 tbsp plain flour
4 pieces of veal shank (*osso bucco*)
2 small onions
30 ml/2 tbsp olive oil
1 large celery stick, finely chopped
1 medium carrot, finely chopped
2 garlic cloves, finely chopped
400g/14 oz can chopped tomatoes
300 ml/½ pint/1¼ cups dry
   white wine
300 ml/½ pint/1¼ cups chicken
   or veal stock
1 strip of thinly pared lemon rind
2 bay leaves, plus extra for
   garnishing
salt and ground black pepper

FOR THE *GREMOLATA*
30ml/2 tbsp finely chopped fresh flat
   leaf parsley
finely grated rind of 1 lemon
1 garlic clove, finely chopped

onions   *celery*   *carrot*   *olive oil*   *canned tomatoes*
bay leaves   *garlic*   *plain flour*
chicken stock   *lemon*   *parsley*   *white wine*

COOK'S TIP
Osso bucco is available from large supermarkets and good butchers. Choose pieces about 2 cm/¾ in thick.

1 Preheat the oven to 160°C/325°F/ Gas 3. Season the flour with salt and pepper and spread it out in a shallow bowl. Add the pieces of veal and turn them in the flour until evenly coated. Shake off any excess flour.

4 Add the chopped tomatoes, wine, stock, lemon rind and bay leaves, then season to taste with salt and pepper. Bring to the boil, stirring.

2 Slice one of the onions into rings. Heat the oil in a large flameproof casserole, then add the veal, with the onion rings, and brown the veal on both sides over a medium heat. Remove the veal with tongs and set aside to drain.

5 Return the veal pieces to the pan and coat thoroughly with the sauce. Cover and cook in the oven for 2 hours or until the veal feels tender when pierced with a fork.

3 Chop the remaining onion and add to the pan with the celery, carrot and garlic. Stir the bottom of the pan to mix in the juices and sediment. Cook gently, stirring frequently, for about 5 minutes until the vegetables soften slightly.

6 Meanwhile, make the *gremolata*. Mix together the parsley, lemon rind and garlic. Remove the casserole from the oven and discard the lemon rind and bay leaves. Taste the sauce for seasoning. Serve hot, sprinkled with the *gremolata* and garnished with extra bay leaves.

Garlic Chicken on a Bed of Vegetables

This is the perfect after-work dinner-party dish: it is quick to prepare and full of sunshiny flavours.

Serves 4

INGREDIENTS

4 chicken breasts, 675 g/1½ lb
    total weight
225 g/8 oz/1 cup soft cheese with
    garlic and herbs
450 g/1 lb courgettes
2 red peppers, seeded
450 g/1 lb plum tomatoes
4 celery sticks
45 ml/3 tbsp olive oil
275 g/10 oz onions,
    roughly chopped
3 garlic cloves, crushed
8 sun-dried tomatoes,
    roughly chopped
5 ml/1 tsp dried oregano
30 ml/2 tbsp balsamic vinegar
5 ml/1 tsp paprika
salt and ground black pepper
olive ciabatta or crusty bread,
    to serve

1 Preheat the oven to 190°C/375°F/ Gas 5. Loosen the skin of each chicken breast, without removing it, to make a pocket. Divide the cheese into quarters and push one quarter underneath the skin of each chicken breast, spreading it in an even layer.

2 Cut the courgettes and peppers into similar-sized chunky pieces. Quarter the tomatoes and slice the celery sticks.

ciabatta loaf

olive oil

plum tomatoes

celery

garlic

chicken breasts

onions

dried oregano

sun-dried tomatoes

soft cheese with garlic and herbs

red peppers

paprika

courgettes

balsamic vinegar

3 Heat 30 ml/2 tbsp of the oil in a large, shallow, flameproof casserole. Cook the onions and garlic for 4 minutes until the onions are soft and golden, stirring frequently.

4 Add the chopped courgettes, peppers and celery and cook for 5 more minutes.

5 Stir in the plum tomatoes, sun-dried tomatoes, oregano and balsamic vinegar. Season well with salt and pepper.

6 Place the chicken on top, drizzle on the remaining olive oil and season with salt and paprika. Bake for 35–40 minutes or until the chicken is golden and cooked through. Serve with plenty of olive ciabatta or crusty bread.

Meat-stuffed Cabbage Rolls

Stuffed cabbage leaves are a good way of using up cooked meats and make a satisfying luncheon dish.

Serves 4–5

INGREDIENTS
1 head Savoy cabbage
75 g/3 oz white bread
a little milk
350 g/12 oz cold cooked meat, very finely chopped, or fresh minced lean beef
1 egg, beaten
30 ml/2 tbsp finely chopped fresh parsley
1 garlic clove, finely chopped
50 g/2 oz/½ cup freshly grated Parmesan cheese
pinch of grated nutmeg
75 ml/5 tbsp olive oil
1 medium onion, finely chopped
250 ml/8 fl oz/1 cup dry white wine
salt and ground black pepper

1 Cut the leaves from the cabbage, reserving the innermost part for a soup. Blanch the leaves, a few at a time, in a large pan of boiling water for 4–5 minutes. Refresh under cold water. Spread the leaves out on clean tea towels to dry.

2 Cut the crust from the bread and discard. Dice the bread and soak it in a little milk for about 5 minutes. Squeeze out the excess moisture with your hands.

white wine

Savoy cabbage

minced beef

milk

egg　　*garlic*

onion

nutmeg

white bread

Parmesan cheese　*olive oil*

parsley

3 In a mixing bowl, combine the chopped or minced meat with the egg and soaked bread. Stir in the parsley, garlic and Parmesan cheese. Season with nutmeg, salt and pepper to taste.

4 Divide any very large cabbage leaves in half, discarding the rib. Lay the leaves out on a flat surface. Form little sausage-shaped mounds of stuffing and place them at the edge of each leaf. Roll up the leaves, tucking the ends in as you roll. Squeeze each roll lightly in the palm of your hand to help the leaves to stick.

VARIATION
Serve the cabbage rolls with a tomato sauce, spooned over just before serving.

5 In a large pan big enough to hold all the rolls in one layer, heat the olive oil. Add the onion and cook gently until it softens. Raise the heat slightly and add the rolls, turning them with a large spoon as they begin to cook.

6 Pour in half the wine. Cook over a low to medium heat until the wine has evaporated. Add the rest of the wine, cover the pan and cook for 10–15 minutes more. Remove the lid and cook until all the liquid has evaporated. Remove from the heat and allow to rest for about 5 minutes before serving.

Baked Lasagne with Meat Sauce

This traditional creamy lasagne is exquisite.

Serves 8–10

INGREDIENTS

1 quantity Bolognese Meat Sauce
 (see Basic Recipes)
400 g/14 oz dried lasagne
115 g/4 oz/1 cup grated
 Parmesan cheese
40 g/1½ oz/3 tbsp butter
salt and ground black pepper

FOR THE BÉCHAMEL SAUCE

750 ml/1¼ pints/3 cups milk
1 bay leaf
3 blades mace
115 g/4 oz/½ cup butter
75 g/3 oz/⅔ cup flour

Bolognese Meat Sauce

lasagne

Parmesan cheese

butter

flour

milk

bay leaf

mace

1 Prepare the meat sauce. Set aside. Butter a large, shallow baking dish. Preheat the oven to 200°C/400°F/Gas 6. Make the béchamel sauce. Heat the milk with the bay leaf and mace in a saucepan. Melt the butter in a separate saucepan.

2 Add the flour to the butter and mix in well with a whisk. Cook for 2–3 minutes. Strain the hot milk into the flour and butter and mix with the whisk. Bring to the boil, stirring constantly, and cook for 4–5 minutes. Season and set aside.

3 Bring a large pan of water to the boil, add salt and half the lasagne sheets. Cook for 4 minutes less than the time recommended on the packet. Cover a large work surface with a clean cloth. Remove the lasagne from the pan and drop into a bowl of cold water for 30 seconds. Remove, and lay them out flat, without overlapping, on the cloth. Repeat for the second batch of lasagne.

6 Bake in the oven for 20 minutes or until brown on top. Remove from the oven and allow to stand for 5 minutes before serving. Serve directly from the baking dish, cutting out rectangular or square sections for each helping.

4 To assemble the lasagne, have all the elements at hand: the baking dish, béchamel and meat sauces, pasta strips, grated Parmesan and butter. Spread one large spoonful of the meat sauce over the bottom of the dish. Arrange a layer of pasta over the meat sauce, cutting it with a sharp knife so that it fits well inside the dish.

5 Cover with a thin layer of meat sauce, then one of béchamel. Sprinkle with a little cheese. Repeat the layers in the same order, ending with a layer of pasta coated with béchamel. Do not make more than about six layers of pasta. Use the pasta trimmings to patch any gaps in the pasta. Sprinkle the top with Parmesan, and dot with butter.

COOK'S TIP

If you have any of the sauces and pasta left over, do not throw them away. Instead, use them to make a small lasagne, layering the pasta and sauce in the same way. If you wish, you can then freeze the lasagne, uncooked, to use another day.

Spaghetti with Meatballs

No Italian menu would be complete without succulent meatballs served on a bed of spaghetti. Serve these with a light green salad and some warm, crusty bread.

Serves 4

INGREDIENTS
350 g/12 oz spaghetti
salt and ground black pepper
fresh rosemary sprigs, to garnish
freshly grated Parmesan cheese,
    to serve

FOR THE MEATBALLS
1 medium onion, chopped
1 garlic clove, chopped
350 g/12 oz minced lamb
1 egg yolk, size 3
15 ml/1 tbsp chopped fresh parsley
15 ml/1 tbsp olive oil

FOR THE SAUCE
300 ml/½ pint/1¼ cups passata (see
    Cook's Tip)
30 ml/2 tbsp chopped fresh basil
1 garlic clove, chopped

spaghetti

rosemary

basil

fresh parsley

Parmesan cheese

onion

egg

garlic

passata

olive oil

minced lamb

1 To make the meatballs, mix together the onion, garlic, lamb, egg yolk, parsley and seasoning until well blended.

2 Divide the mixture into 20 pieces and mould into balls. Place on a baking sheet, cover with clear film and chill for 30 minutes.

3 Heat the oil in a large frying pan and place the meatballs in it.

4 Fry the meatballs for about 10 minutes, turning occasionally, until browned on all sides. Drain the pan of any excess fat, without tipping the meatballs out.

5 For the sauce, add the passata, basil, garlic and seasoning to the pan and bring to the boil. Cover and simmer for 20 minutes until the meatballs are tender.

COOK'S TIP

Passata is available in jars, tins or cartons from specialist Italian grocery stores and most large supermarkets. It is made from sieved tomatoes, so if you cannot find any, drain and sieve canned tomatoes instead.

The meatballs can be made a day in advance. Place them on a baking sheet, cover with clear film and chill.

6 Meanwhile, bring a large pan of salted water to the boil. Add the pasta and cook according to the packet instructions until it is just *al dente*. Drain thoroughly and divide it among four serving plates. Spoon over the meatballs and some of the sauce. Garnish each portion with a fresh rosemary sprig and serve immediately with plenty of freshly grated Parmesan cheese.

Pasta with Spring Vegetables

This delicious vegetarian dish is perfect for a light lunch or supper.

Serves 4

INGREDIENTS
115 g/4 oz broccoli florets
115 g/4 oz baby leeks
225 g/8 oz asparagus
1 small fennel bulb
115 g/4 oz fresh or frozen peas
40 g/1½ oz/3 tbsp butter
1 shallot, chopped
45 ml/3 tbsp chopped fresh mixed
    herbs, such as parsley, thyme
    and sage
300 ml/½ pint/1¼ cups
    double cream
350 g/12 oz dried penne pasta
salt and ground black pepper
freshly grated Parmesan cheese,
    to serve

peas

broccoli

butter

double cream

penne

Parmesan cheese

mixed herbs

shallot

baby leeks

asparagus

fennel

1 Divide the broccoli florets into tiny sprigs. Cut the leeks and asparagus diagonally into 5 cm/2 in lengths. Trim the fennel bulb and remove any tough outer leaves. Cut into wedges, leaving the layers attached at the root ends so that the pieces stay intact.

2 Cook each prepared vegetable, including the peas, separately in boiling salted water until just tender – use the same water for each vegetable. Drain well and keep warm.

3 Melt the butter in a separate pan, add the chopped shallot and cook, stirring occasionally, until softened but not browned. Stir in the herbs and cream and cook for a few minutes until slightly thickened. Meanwhile, bring a large pan of salted water to the boil.

4 Add the pasta to the boiling water and cook according to the packet instructions until it is just *al dente*. Drain well and add to the sauce with the vegetables. Toss gently and season with plenty of pepper. Serve hot with a sprinkling of freshly grated Parmesan.

Tagliatelle with Mushrooms

The mushroom sauce is quick to make and the pasta cooks very quickly; both need to be cooked as near to serving as possible, so careful co-ordination is required.

Serves 4

INGREDIENTS

about 50 g/2 oz/4 tbsp butter
225–350 g/8–12 oz chanterelles
15 ml/1 tbsp plain flour
150 ml/¼ pint/⅔ cup milk
90 ml/6 tbsp crème fraîche
15 ml/1 tbsp chopped fresh parsley
275 g/10 oz fresh or dried tagliatelle
olive oil, for tossing
salt and ground black pepper

butter

flour

chanterelles

milk

crème fraîche

parsley

olive oil

tagliatelle

COOK'S TIP
Chanterelles are a little tricky to wash, as they are so delicate. However, since these are woodland mushrooms, it's important to clean them thoroughly. Hold each one by the stalk and let cold water run under the gills to dislodge hidden dirt. Shake gently to dry.

1 Melt 40 g/1½ oz/3 tbsp of the butter in a frying pan and fry the mushrooms for about 2–3 minutes over a gentle heat until the juices begin to run, then increase the heat and cook until the liquid has almost evaporated. Transfer the cooked mushrooms to a bowl using a slotted spoon.

2 Stir in the flour, adding a little more butter if necessary, and cook for about 1 minute, then gradually stir in the milk to make a smooth sauce.

3 Add the crème fraîche, mushrooms and parsley and seasoning and stir well. Cook very gently to heat through and then keep warm while cooking the pasta.

4 Bring a large pan of salted water to the boil. Add the pasta and cook according to the packet instructions until it is just *al dente*. Drain well, toss in a little olive oil and then turn on to a warmed serving plate. Pour the mushroom sauce over and serve immediately whilst it is hot.

VARIATION
If chanterelles are unavailable, use other wild mushrooms of your choice.

Baked Seafood Spaghetti

In this dish, each portion is baked and served in an individual packet which is then opened at the table. Use baking parchment or aluminium foil to make the packets.

Serves 4

INGREDIENTS

450 g/1 lb mussels, in their shells
120 ml/4 fl oz/½ cup dry white wine
60 ml/4 tbsp olive oil
2 garlic cloves, finely chopped
450 g/1 lb tomatoes, peeled and
    finely chopped
400 g/14 oz spaghetti or other
    long pasta
225 g/8 oz uncooked prawns,
    peeled and deveined
30 ml/2 tbsp chopped fresh parsley
salt and ground black pepper

mussels   *white wine*

olive oil

tomatoes

garlic   *spaghetti*

prawns   *parsley*

1 Scrub the mussels well under cold running water, cutting off the "beards" with a small, sharp knife. Place the mussels and the wine in a large saucepan and heat until the mussels open.

2 Lift out the mussels and set aside. (Discard any that do not open.) Strain the cooking liquid through kitchen paper and reserve until needed. Preheat the oven to 150°C/300°F/Gas 2.

3 In a medium saucepan, heat the oil and garlic together for 1–2 minutes. Add the tomatoes and cook over a medium to high heat until they soften. Stir in 150 ml/6 fl oz/¾ cup of the cooking liquid from the mussels. Bring a large pan of salted water to the boil. Add the pasta and cook according to the packet instructions until it is just *al dente*.

4 Just before draining the pasta, add the prawns and the chopped parsley to the tomato sauce. Cook for 2 minutes or until the prawns are stiff. Taste one and adjust the seasoning if necessary, then remove from the heat.

5 Prepare four pieces of baking parchment or foil about 30 x 45 cm/ 12 x 18 in. Place each sheet in the centre of a shallow bowl. (The bowl under the paper will stop the sauce from spilling while the paper parcels are being closed.) Turn the drained pasta into a bowl. Add the tomato sauce and mix well. Stir in the mussels.

COOK'S TIP

Bottled mussels or clams may be substituted for fresh shellfish in this recipe: add them to the tomato sauce with the prawns. Canned tomatoes may be used instead of fresh ones.

6 Divide the pasta and seafood between the four pieces of paper, placing a mound in the centre of each and twisting the paper ends together to make a closed packet. Arrange on a large baking sheet and place in the centre of the oven. Bake for 8–10 minutes. Place one unopened packet on each individual serving plate.

Pasta with Tomato Sauce and Roasted Vegetables

Roasting the vegetables at a high temperature concentrates their flavours wonderfully for a sauce that almost oozes sunshine.

Serves 4

INGREDIENTS
1 aubergine
2 courgettes
1 large onion
2 red or yellow peppers, seeded
450 g/1 lb tomatoes
2–3 garlic cloves,
    coarsely chopped
50 ml/2 fl oz/¼ cup olive oil
250 ml/8 fl oz/1 cup Tomato Sauce
    for Pasta (see Basic Recipes)
50 g/2 oz/⅓ cup black olives,
    halved and stoned
350–450 g/12 oz–1 lb dried pasta
    shapes, such as rigatoni or penne
45 ml/3 tbsp shredded fresh basil
salt and ground black pepper
freshly grated Parmesan cheese,
    to serve (optional)

courgettes
aubergine
onion
black olives
tomatoes
olive oil
basil
garlic
penne

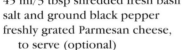
Basic Tomato Sauce
Parmesan cheese
peppers

1 Preheat the oven to 240°C/475°F/ Gas 9. Cut the aubergine, courgettes, onion, peppers and tomatoes into 4 cm/1½ in chunks. Discard all the tomato seeds.

2 Spread out the vegetables in a large roasting tin. Sprinkle the garlic and oil over the vegetables and stir and turn to mix evenly. Season with salt and pepper.

3 Roast the vegetables in the oven for about 30 minutes until they are soft and browned (don't worry if the edges are charred black). Stir half-way through the cooking time.

4 Scrape the vegetable mixture into a saucepan. Add the tomato sauce and the halved olives.

5 Bring a large pan of salted water to the boil. Add the pasta and cook according to the packet instructions until it is just *al dente*.

6 Meanwhile, heat the tomato and roasted vegetable sauce, stirring occasionally. Taste and adjust the seasoning if necessary.

7 Drain the pasta and return it to the pan. Add the tomato and roasted vegetable sauce and mix to combine well. Serve hot, sprinkled with the shredded basil. If desired, sprinkle with freshly grated Parmesan cheese.

Pizza Margarita

This classic pizza is simple to prepare once you have the basics in store. The sweet flavour of sun-ripe tomatoes works wonderfully with the basil and mozzarella.

Serves 2–3

INGREDIENTS
1 pizza base, 25–30 cm/10–12 in
    diameter (see Basic Recipes)
30 ml/2 tbsp olive oil
1 quantity Basic Tomato Sauce
    for Pizzas (see Basic Recipes)
150 g/5 oz mozzarella cheese
2 ripe tomatoes, thinly sliced
6–8 fresh basil leaves
30 ml/2 tbsp freshly grated
    Parmesan cheese
ground black pepper

basil

*olive
oil*

mozzarella

tomatoes

*Parmesan
cheese*

*Basic
Tomato
Sauce*

*pizza
base*

1 Preheat the oven to 220°C/425°F/ Gas 7. Brush the pizza base with 15 ml/ 1 tbsp of the oil and then spread over the tomato sauce, leaving a small border around the edge of the base.

2 Using a sharp knife, cut the mozzarella cheese into thin slices.

3 Arrange the sliced mozzarella and tomatoes on top of the tomato sauce on the pizza base.

4 Roughly tear the basil leaves and sprinkle them over the pizza with the Parmesan cheese. Drizzle over the remaining oil and season with pepper. Bake for 15–20 minutes until crisp and golden. Serve immediately.

Quattro Stagioni Pizza

This traditional pizza is divided into quarters, each with a different topping to depict the four seasons of the year.

Serves 2–4

INGREDIENTS
45 ml/3 tbsp olive oil
50 g/2 oz/1 cup button
    mushrooms, sliced
1 pizza base, 25–30 cm/10–12 in
    diameter (see Basic Recipes)
1 quantity Basic Tomato Sauce
    for Pizzas (see Basic Recipes)
50 g/2 oz Parma ham
6 black olives, stoned and chopped
4 bottled artichoke hearts in
    oil, drained
3 canned anchovy fillets, drained
50 g/2 oz mozzarella cheese,
    thinly sliced
8 fresh basil leaves, shredded
ground black pepper

artichoke hearts   *mozzarella cheese*   *basil*

Parma ham

black olives

pizza base

Basic Tomato Sauce   *anchovy fillets*   *button mushrooms*   *olive oil*

1 Preheat the oven to 220°C/425°F/ Gas 7. Heat 15 ml/1 tbsp of the oil in a frying pan and fry the mushrooms until all the juices have evaporated. Leave the mushrooms to cool.

2 Brush the pizza base with half the remaining oil. Spread over the tomato sauce and mark into four equal sections with a knife.

3 Arrange the mushrooms over one section of the pizza.

4 Cut the Parma ham into thin strips and arrange the strips with the olives on another section of the pizza.

5 Thinly slice the artichoke hearts and arrange over a third section. Halve the anchovies lengthways and arrange with the mozzarella over the fourth section.

COOK'S TIP

You can use your imagination for the four toppings for this pizza. Try adding seafood such as cooked clams, mussels or prawns for one quarter, broccoli florets for another, roasted peppers for another and roasted onions and garlic for the rest.

6 Scatter over the basil. Drizzle over the remaining oil and season with pepper. Bake for 15–20 minutes until crisp and golden. Serve immediately, cut into slices.

Pepperoni Pizza

This popular pizza is spiced with green chillies and pepperoni. You can make this dish less hot by omitting some of the chillies.

Serves 2–3

INGREDIENTS

1 pizza base, 25–30 cm/10–12 in
   diameter (see Basic Recipes)
15 ml/1 tbsp olive oil
115 g/4 oz can peeled and chopped
   green chillies in brine, drained
1 quantity Basic Tomato Sauce for
   Pizzas (see Basic Recipes)
75 g/3 oz sliced pepperoni
8–10 black olives, stoned
15 ml/1 tbsp chopped fresh oregano
115 g/4 oz mozzarella cheese,
   grated
fresh oregano leaves, to garnish

black olives *green chillies* *pepperoni*

Basic Tomato Sauce *mozzarella cheese* *olive oil*

oregano *pizza base*

I Preheat the oven to 220°C/425°F/ Gas 7. Brush the pizza base with the oil.

2 Stir the chopped green chillies into the tomato sauce, and spread the sauce over the pizza base.

3 Arrange the sliced pepperoni over the tomato sauce on the pizza base.

4 Halve the olives lengthways and scatter them over the pepperoni with the oregano.

5 Sprinkle over the grated mozzarella and bake for 15–20 minutes until the pizza is crisp and golden.

6 Garnish with fresh oregano leaves and serve immediately.

VARIATION

You can make this pizza as hot as you like. For a really fiery version use fresh red or green chillies, cut into thin slices, in place of the chillies in brine.

Choux Pastries with Two Custards

Italian pastry shops are filled with displays of sweetly scented pastries such as these.

Makes about 48

INGREDIENTS
200 ml/7 fl oz/scant 1 cup water
115 g/4 oz/½ cup butter
2.5 cm/1 in piece vanilla pod
150 g/5 oz/1¼ cups plain flour
5 eggs
pinch of salt

FOR THE CUSTARD FILLINGS
50 g/2 oz plain cooking chocolate
300 ml/½ pint/1¼ cups milk
4 egg yolks
65 g/2½ oz/scant ⅓ cup
    granulated sugar
40 g/1½ oz/generous ⅓ cup flour
5 ml/1 tsp pure vanilla extract
300 ml/½ pint/1¼ cups
    whipping cream
unsweetened cocoa powder and
    icing sugar, for dusting

butter   eggs

granulated
sugar

vanilla
pod
    plain
cooking chocolate   icing sugar

water   cocoa
    powder

milk

vanilla
extract

flour   whipping
    cream

1 Preheat the oven to 190°C/375°F/ Gas 5. Heat the water with the butter, vanilla pod and salt. When the butter has melted, beat in the flour.

2 Cook over low heat, stirring constantly, for about 8 minutes. Remove from the heat. Beat in the eggs one at a time. Remove the vanilla pod.

3 Butter a baking sheet. Using a piping bag fitted with a round nozzle, squeeze the mixture out on to the sheet in balls the size of small walnuts, leaving space between the rows to allow for spreading. Bake for 20–25 minutes or until the pastries are golden brown. Remove from the oven and allow to cool thoroughly before filling.

4 Meanwhile, prepare the custard fillings. Melt the cooking chocolate in the top half of a double boiler, or in a bowl set over a pan of simmering water. Heat the milk in a small saucepan over a gentle to moderate heat, taking care not to let it boil.

5 Beat the egg yolks with a wire whisk or electric beater. Gradually add the sugar and continue beating until the mixture is pale yellow. Beat in the flour. Add the hot milk very gradually, pouring it in through a sieve. When all the milk has been added, pour the mixture into a medium heavy-based saucepan and bring to the boil. Simmer for 5–6 minutes, stirring.

Zabaglione

A much-loved, simple Italian pudding traditionally made with Marsala, an Italian fortified wine. Madeira is a good alternative.

Serves 4

INGREDIENTS
4 egg yolks
50 g/2 oz/4 tbsp caster sugar
60 ml/4 tbsp Marsala or
  Madeira wine
amaretti biscuits, to serve

eggs

caster sugar

Marsala

amaretti biscuits

1 Place the egg yolks and caster sugar in a large, clean, heatproof bowl and whisk with an electric beater until the mixture is pale and thick and forms fluffy peaks when the whisk is lifted out of the eggs.

2 Gradually add the Marsala or Madeira, whisking well after each addition (at this stage the mixture will be quite runny).

3 Now place over a pan of gently simmering water and continue to whisk for at least 5–7 minutes until the mixture becomes thick and mousse-like; when the beaters are lifted, they should leave a thick trail on the surface of the mixture.

4 Pour into four warmed, stemmed glasses and serve immediately with the amaretti biscuits for dipping.

COOK'S TIP
Make sure the zabaglione is thick and mousse-like: if you don't beat the mixture for long enough, the zabaglione will be too runny and will probably separate.

VARIATION
If you don't have any Marsala or Madeira, you could use a medium-sweet sherry or a dessert wine.

Stuffed Peaches with Mascarpone Cream

Mascarpone is a thick, velvety Italian cream cheese, made from cow's milk. It is often used in desserts, or eaten with fresh fruit.

Serves 4

INGREDIENTS
4 large peaches, halved and stoned
40 g/1½ oz amaretti biscuits,
    crumbled
30 ml/2 tbsp ground almonds
45 ml/3 tbsp sugar
15 ml/1 tbsp cocoa powder
150 ml/¼ pint/⅔ cup sweet wine
25 g/1 oz/2 tbsp butter

FOR THE MASCARPONE CREAM
30 ml/2 tbsp caster sugar
3 egg yolks
15 ml/1 tbsp sweet wine
225 g/8 oz/1 cup mascarpone
    cheese
150 ml/¼ pint/⅔ cup double cream

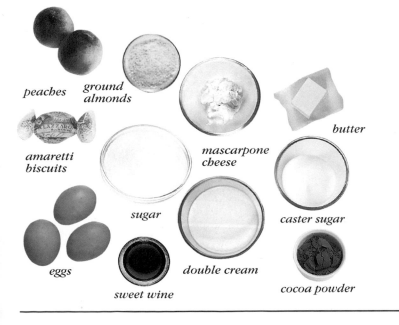

peaches
ground almonds
amaretti biscuits
mascarpone cheese
butter
sugar
caster sugar
eggs
double cream
sweet wine
cocoa powder

1 Preheat the oven to 200°C/400°F/ Gas 6. Using a teaspoon, scoop some of the flesh from the cavities in the peaches, to make a reasonable space for stuffing. Chop the scooped-out flesh.

2 Mix together the amaretti biscuits, ground almonds, sugar, cocoa and peach flesh. Add enough wine to make the mixture into a thick paste. Place the peaches in a buttered ovenproof dish and fill them with the amaretti and almond stuffing. Dot with butter, then pour the remaining wine into the dish. Bake for 35 minutes.

3 To make the mascarpone cream, beat the caster sugar and egg yolks until thick and pale. Stir in the wine, then fold in the mascarpone. Whip the double cream to soft peaks and fold into the mixture. Remove the peaches from the oven and leave to cool. Serve the peaches at room temperature, with the mascarpone cream.

INDEX